Total Sports Conditioning for Athletes 50+

Total Sports Conditioning for Athletes 50+

Workouts for Staying at the Top of Your Game

DR. KARL KNOPF

photography by Andy Mogg

Ulysses Press

Published in the United States by Ulysses Press
P.O. Box 3440
Berkeley, CA 94703
www.ulyssespress.com

ISBN10: 1-56975-647-3
ISBN13: 978-1-56975-647-8
Library of Congress Control Number 2007907768

Printed in Canada by Webcom

10 9 8 7 6 5 4 3 2 1

Editorial/Production	Lily Chou, Claire Chun, Lauren Harrison, Tamara Kowalski, Judith Metzener, Steven Zah Schwartz
Index	Sayre Van Young
Cover design	what!design @ whatweb.com
Cover photographs	© iStockphoto.com
Interior photographs	© Andy Mogg, except on pages 2, 4, 8 and 19 © iStockphoto.com; pages 113–30 © Robert Holmes
Models	Karl Knopf, Toni Silver, Jacques Rutschmann, Vivian Gunderson, Michael O'Meara, Phyllis Ritchie

Distributed by Publishers Group West

Please Note

This book has been written and published strictly for informational purposes, and in
no way should be used as a substitute for consultation with health care professionals. You should not consider educational material herein to be the practice of medicine or to replace consultation with a physician or other medical practitioner. The
author and publisher are providing you with information in this work so that you
can have the knowledge and can choose, at your own risk, to act on that knowledge. The author and publisher also urge all readers to be aware of their health status and to consult health care professionals before beginning any health program.

contents

part 1:
overview

forever fit

In the United States, people are staying younger longer and engaging in active lifestyles like never before. The mantra of today's older adult is "Life begins at 50." We're in better health, are better educated, and are wealthier than any previous middle-age generation. The 50-plus age group goes by many names—"baby boomer," "older American," "mature adult," "retiree," while some prefer to be called "master athlete" or "vintage athlete." Our group is not satisfied by living on past achievements. We're looking for new challenges physically, academically, and socially.

Today's master athletes are seeking far more than an exercise program that improves their health or physique—they desire a challenging exercise program that will help them cultivate the way they function in everyday activities as well as how they function while playing. As one master athlete said, "Life is not a journey to the grave with the intention of arriving safely, with a pretty and well-preserved body, but rather to skid in broadside, thoroughly used up, totally worn out, and loudly proclaiming, WOW, what a ride!"

Many master athletes are revisiting the games and sports they were devoted to in their youth, while some are discovering new recreational activities: fun runs, century bike rides, triathlons, open-water swims, track and field, basketball, softball. Age, gender, and even physical limitations pose no barrier. Proper training and good equipment will allow master athletes to enjoy their sport as long as their passion exists.

Join the ranks of those who understand that age is no excuse to be sedentary and weak. Age is just the number—what's more important is how you feel, how you act, and how you play. Most of us don't want to live long to only survive—we want to thrive and enjoy a fulfilling quality of life. In fact, a private secret that numerous master athletes have is that they can't wait for their next birthday so they can move up a category to compete against a different group.

Total Sports Conditioning for Athletes 50+ strives to present techniques to foster better health and wellness and, more importantly, to provide some training tips that will allow you to continue competing as you age and help you preserve and improve your sports performance. You'll learn how to train smart and not get hurt so that you can truly age to perfection.

Author Karl Knopf (right) makes some adjustments.

the perks of play

On the journey of life, the road to health and wellness is determined by the daily choices we make. Good choices make the road smooth, uneventful, and satisfying, and more Americans than ever before are enjoying longer rides. In 2000, there were 120 million Americans 40 years and older. By the year 2020, there will be 160 million Americans who are 40 plus. The 85-plus age group is swelling but the centenarians are the fastest-growing group.

The Centers for Disease Control attributes this increased longevity to the reduction of six of the fifteen leading causes of death, most notably heart disease, cancer, stroke, the flu, liver disease, and accidents. With improved antibiotics, water quality, and sanitation, life expectancy has improved. In the 1880s, people died in childbirth and from pneumonia. Today, we're dying from the consequences of too much food and inactivity.

Countless older adults are rusting out long before they wear out. Much of what we associate with aging is really the culmination of misuse, disuse, and abuse of our bodies. This can be the result of poor health habits, inactivity, or simply overdoing it. A multitude of people age as a result of disusing their bodies, perhaps living a sedentary, zoo-like existence in front of the TV or computer; these people suffer from hypokinetic disease or couch potato syndrome. Misusing their bodies can also hasten the aging process; this misuse is usually the by-product of chronic and habitual improper body mechanics while playing or working. The people who are aging faster than most are doing so by abusing their internal systems, either through smoking, drinking, or eating excessively.

Our objective in our golden years should be to increase

both our life span and our health span. Most of us know what life span is but most people are not familiar with health span. Health span includes being more energetic, being more flexible, and being able to enjoy life more fully. Simply put, it's being fit for life and for the challenges and demands presented by it. Staying active can halt the damage of normal aging and perhaps even reverse it.

Professional athletes in just about every sport attain their peak in their late 20s, with the onset of decline occurring in their early 30s. Many sports such as baseball require a complex combination of many skills. Speed in these sports peaks around the age of 23, while power tops out at age 26. In general, power wanes sooner and more dramatically than endurance, with most athletes showing some loss in their early 30s. Endurance performance peaks for men in their 20s, declining by about four percent between the ages of 25 and 55; women peak in their 30s, although their strength and power show a faster decline.

In normal aging, we decline about two percent a year;

active and fit people age at about half a percent. Multiply two percent versus half a percent over 30 years and that decline can be the difference between remaining independent and being confined to a wheelchair or nursing home. As we age, we lose about six to eight percent in relative power. Power declines to a greater degree than strength over time, and it accelerates even faster after the age of 60. Flexibility declines about five percent each decade, which can lead to impaired balance and difficulty in doing simple things like tying your shoes. After 70, we experience a significant loss of aerobic ability.

Don't despair, though. How we age is largely influenced by how we live. Our longevity is in our hands: 30 percent of it lies in our genes, leaving 70 percent up to us. We have the knowledge to make a significant change in our quality— and quantity—of life, and what we do today will determine how we live tomorrow. The fountain of youth has been discovered. It's not in a bottle, in an injection, or in a pill. It's found in a daily dose of sensible physical activity. Research shows that, with proper exer-

A national study found that women are generally *happier* after 50 and reach their peak of satisfaction with life in their 70s.

cise and nutrition, fit 60-year-olds can retain 80 percent of the strength they had when they were 25. Just walking briskly can slow down the effects of aging and can improve aerobic capacity by 15 to 20 percent. Lifting weights two to three times a week for 20 minutes can recapture strength and rebuild muscle. Engaging in power training minimizes losses in power while proper sports conditioning can bring back strength and functional ability.

The sport-specific exercise programs in Part 2 will further help you improve and/or maintain your physical abilities. They'll also contribute to a positive self-image, foster better quality of sleep, enhance bone density, and assist in weight control.

what is total sports conditioning?

We've all envied athletes who move effortlessly when performing their sport. The goal of sports conditioning is to help all athletes move in a similar manner no matter what our age. Fitness training, while good for health, will not elevate your sports skill to the next level.

The primary difference between fitness training and sports conditioning is that fitness training is more general and less intense than sports conditioning. Training for a sport requires specificity of training, which means if you want to be a better swimmer, you need to perform tasks that are directly related to the muscles that are engaged in the activity of swimming.

Every motion or exercise performed in a sports conditioning program should replicate those activities performed within the sport or activity, and should also be as useful, safe and effective as possible. Sports conditioning is simply another application of SAID, or Specific Adaptation to Imposed Demands. This means that muscles will adapt to specific demands placed upon them. Therefore, if you want to learn to run faster, you must do activities that engage the fast-twitch muscle fibers. A SAID exercise that most sprinters perform involves doing sprints, resting and repeating. On the other hand, marathon runners must engage in LSD, or long slow distance, which specifically trains slow-twitch muscle fibers to contract and relax over a prolonged period of time. The bottom line is that sports conditioning is exercise with a purpose.

Perhaps you're one of the many 50-plus athletes who've attempted this kind of training but are reluctant to give it another try because you injured yourself in the process. If you followed protocols laid out in magazines, you should know that the majority of those conditioning programs are geared toward younger athletes; thus, they include many ballistic and high-impact moves that are not worth the risk for mature athletes. Or perhaps you've been incorporating outdated principles you learned in college or while in the service when you were 20 years old. The younger body is more tolerant of biomechanical errors. The more mature body must be treated like a vintage car if you don't want it to break down.

Fitness and exercise science have evolved significantly over the years, but many of the principles and training methods used in the gym today are still dominated by the bodybuilding principles of the old Muscle Beach days. The whole point of bodybuilding was to enhance the way muscles appeared; it was not about how the muscles functioned. Often when we train to make muscles bigger, we often create muscle imbalances that lead to chronic injury. In addition, these old principles neglected the deep-lying muscles of the body, focusing on the primary muscles but not the stabilizers, which hold a body part in position while other parts are moving.

In many cases the way we train muscles in the gym is not at all related to the functions that those muscles perform out in the real world. For instance, some evidence suggests that doing weight-bearing exercises such as leg extensions have no real carryover benefit to running and jumping. *Total Sports Conditioning for Athletes 50+* presents functional moves that have been used successfully and safely by many vintage athletes. By training muscular patterns for specific tasks, you'll improve your overall performance.

principles of training

Training for sports takes time. Scientific research has concluded that it takes a minimum of ten years or 10,000 hours to reach elite athlete status. That equates to three hours of training a day. Over the past decade, sports conditioning has evolved more into a science rather than just spending time performing the sport and learning strategies. Today, training to play requires a whole new set of training concepts, from physiological aspects to motivational skills as well as techniques such as plyometrics and multijoint lifts, and power training and speed and agility work.

The role of your exercise program should be to foster functional fitness for life and sport. However, the human body is a delicate machine. Without a basic understanding of this machine, it's doomed to break down. This section provides the essential information needed to train smart and obtain optimal results.

Bones are functional levers that connect to one another, forming numerous types of joints in the human body. They're attached with ligaments (bone to bone) and/or tendons (bone to muscle). Some joints are fused together, such as in the skull; others are hinged joints, such as in the elbow; and yet others are called the ball and socket joint, as seen in the hip.

Flexibility is the ability of the joint to move freely and comfortably through a complete range of motion. A moderate amount of flexibility is necessary in most sports and is critical in the game of life.

Muscles are the movers and shakers of the body, the pulleys that make the bones move. Muscular strength is the amount of weight/force a muscle can exert, while muscular endurance is the ability of a muscle to contract for a prolonged period of time. In any conditioning program, your muscles will undergo a series of different contractions in order to produce movement. Moving your arms through water, for instance, is a form of *isokinetic contraction*; resistance stays constant throughout the full range of motion. *Isometric contraction* is when no movement occurs because the resistance is constant, such as when you press your hands together in front of your chest. (Note that vintage athletes or anyone with a history of cardiovascular disease, especially high blood pressure, should avoid isometric exercises because they increase blood pressure.)

There are two types of *isotonic contraction*, when the muscle lengthens and shortens: concentric contraction and eccentric contraction. When you raise a glass of water to your mouth, you're performing a concentric contraction of the bicep, i.e., the muscle shortens. Lowering the glass of water to the table creates an eccentric contraction of the bicep, i.e., the muscle lengthens.

Muscles play many roles. Sometimes a muscle is called upon to act independently, while many other times a mus-

cle performs as part of a team, which is most often the case in sports performance. When a muscle acts in an independent fashion, it's called the agonist, or prime mover. The muscle that has an opposite action of the agonist is called the antagonist muscle. In general, your muscles are designed with opposing pairs, featuring both agonist and antagonist muscles. For movements to be smooth and fluid, other muscles are called upon to help or to eliminate unwanted movement. These helpers are called synergists and accessory muscles.

Isolated exercises target muscles in one particular plane. Although they're often performed in fitness routines, they contribute little to sports performance. *Compound exercises* incorporate various muscles and apply greatly to sports performance. As your fitness level improves, you should make an effort to include more compound exercises and reduce the number of isolated exercises. If you can include compound exercises that replicate your particular sport, you're well ahead of the competition.

Proper training with weights or elastic bands is called progressive resistance training, commonly referred to as "strength training." When you

engage in this type of training, the muscles you train will become more toned or even stronger; oftentimes the muscles will hypertrophy, or increase in size. If you stop training, your muscles will atrophy, or decrease in size. The key to successful progres-

PROPER EXERCISE PROGRESSIONS FOR SPORTS CONDITIONING

- A functional sports conditioning program should utilize the following progression:
- Engage large muscles before focusing on small ones.
- Perform simple movements correctly before moving on to complex ones.
- Learn to control static movements before moving on to dynamic activities.
- Perform movements in a slow, controlled manner before progressing to fast movements.
- Perform low-force movements before doing high-force activities.
- Learn to do dual-arm and/or -leg motions prior to doing single-arm and/or -leg movements.
- Understand how to do movements correctly in a single plane prior to performing exercises in multiple planes.
- Focus on doing exercises correctly on a stable surface prior to doing movements on an unstable surface.
- Most importantly, quality movements supercede the quantity of movements. (It takes longer to unlearn a bad habit than it does to learn it correctly the first time.)

TRAINING VARIABLES

Designing a sports conditioning program is much like crafting a fine wine: it requires patience and skill in addition to adding and subtracting the correct ingredients until the proper combination meets your desired outcome. A training session can be similarly adapted and modified—simply tweak the elements of the training session.

- **Repetitions** (reps) are the number of times a movement is repeated.
- **Set** is a grouping of repetitions.
- **Frequency** is the number of times, or intervals, a program is executed. The number of times a week you work out is an example of how frequency is used in training.
- **Intensity** is the overload necessary to promote the desired outcome. Consider the amount of weight you lift or how hard you sprint a quarter-mile.
- **Duration** is the length of each training section.
- **Recovery** can be the time between sets or the time between workouts. The critical question with recovery is how much time is needed for the body to recover and repair itself before it starts to de-condition. There is much controversy about whether or not a person can exercise every day. The answer lies in the intensity of the workout and the make-up of the individual. A person can perform "active rest" by cross-training, or doing a different type of exercise on alternating days.
- **Overload** involves loading the muscles beyond normal capacity to promote increase in muscular strength and/or endurance.
- **Progression** is the process of changing the challenges placed upon the body to stimulate the desired gains. The progression can be adapted by changes to the intensity, volume, frequency, etc., of the training routine.

sive resistance training is to, as your muscles get stronger, increase the load to further challenge them.

Most sports skills rely on *power*, which is a combination of strength and speed applied over a short period of time. In sports, power is used to generate force. Power training incorporates concentric and eccentric contractions and is generally considered more important in sports training than in fitness training. Having big muscles does not automatically translate into a more

forceful tennis serve. In this case, force is generated by having adequate flexibility to extend the arm and then recruit all the muscles of the torso, legs and arms at the proper moment to produce the serve.

Plyometric exercise is an example of power. Plyometrics are a series of exercises that maximize the stretch reflexes to teach muscles to produce maximum force. Plyometrics usually utilize movements such as hopping and jumping, which means they're very traumatic to the body and can

cause overuse injuries in some athletes. Plyometric routines should be used cautiously and not overdone.

Specificity of training involves matching the physical training program to the specific demands required by the sport. In other words, if you play golf, you train by doing an activity that mimics the golf swing, adding resistance or other variables to challenge yourself. Keep in mind, however, that only perfect practice makes perfect.

Cross-training employs a variety of training methods to stimulate a training effect without increasing the risk of injury. A positive example of cross-training is when a runner hits the road on a bike or takes one or two workouts into the pool to perform deep-water running. This allows the cardiovascular system to maintain its conditioning while letting the skeletal system rest. It also prevents injuries that stem from overtraining.

Overtraining occurs when a training routine exceeds the capabilities of the athlete, creating deleterious outcomes to the trainee. Overtraining takes many shapes, from injuries to personality changes to extreme weight loss. The key is to train, not strain.

Periodization is a systematic

approach of changing your training routine at a regularly scheduled interval in order to avoid overtraining. It includes macro and micro cycles that can be tweaked according to your competition schedule. The goal of periodization is to "peak" in time for season competition. This approach allows for year-round training without causing overuse syndrome. A common example is when swimmers go from swimming a long course to short course. The biggest mistake some athletes make is leaving their best performance on the practice field.

Cardiovascular endurance is the capacity to continue physical performance over an extended period of time. While moderate exercise has been shown to lower the risk of heart disease and obesity, new research is showing that more vigorous workouts can ramp up the benefits even more. (Of course, always check with your health provider that you are fit enough to increase the intensity since this increase is usually accompanied by a greater risk of injury.) Researchers from Duke University define vigorous exercise as working at 60 percent or more of your aerobic capacity.

Another safe method to determine aerobic intensity is

A simple method to calculate aerobic intensity is the target heart rate (THR) formula.*
- 220 – your age – your resting heart rate x 60-80% = X
- X + resting heart rate = your target heart rate for 1 minute.

Example: Let's say you're 60 years old with a resting heart rate of 75.
- 220 – 60 – 75 x .65 = 55.25
- 55.25 + 75 = 130.25

Therefore, the target heart rate per minute for this individual is 130, or approximately 20 beats for 10 seconds.

* Note that certain medications such as beta-blockers will "cap" your heart rate so this method is not to be used with those individuals. Also consult with your personal medical doctor for proper training levels.

the "talk test": If you can't talk while training, the intensity is too difficult.

LSD, or long slow duration/ distance, is an effective way to maintain good health and maintain proper body weight. LSD can be any activity, such as walking, biking or swimming, that engages the major muscles of the body for a prolonged period of time.

Reversibility is what happens when you stop using your muscles—you lose all the work that you've done. Basically, your body starts to de-condition about every 72 hours you go without physical activity.

Flexibility, an often-neglected aspect of proper training, is the ability of your

muscles to move through a comfortable and complete range of motion. It helps you generate greater force in a golf swing and is highly recommended for injury prevention. Poor range of motion can impair function and increase muscle pain.

Balance is a critical aspect in many sports and games. Two major components of balance are static balance and dynamic balance. Static balance involves standing in one place while dynamic balance requires maintaining your balance as you move from one location to another. Athletics often requires adequate levels of dynamic balance.

Sports training workouts should be used to improve performance and physical conditioning, not to show off or compete. A quality workout is far superior to a hard but sloppy workout. Train for flexibility, balance, coordination, reaction time, and power—not just strength.

Becoming a Top Performer

To become a top athlete, you must possess several characteristics: inherent natural abilities, physical fitness and motor fitness skills, psychological stamina, skill set. However, if you weren't blessed with natural abilities, you can focus on the other characteristics and still be an outstanding performer. For instance, motor fitness skills, such as hand/foot-eye coordination, speed, power and balance, can be improved vastly with sound training. Also, training specific skills is important as well. We often see that the biggest/fastest/strongest person is not always the winner—it doesn't matter how big your biceps are if you can't hit the ball.

Given that these are the basics to being successful in sports, there's not much you can do to enhance what nature did not bestow upon you. That's not to say there's anything wrong with just "playing" your sport for the health and fun of it. However, if your goal is to compete, your mindset and training will take on another dimension. If you understand the concepts displayed in the pyramid on this page, your chances of performing to your personal best and not getting injured is enhanced.

FOUNDATION OF HEALTH AND FITNESS   The bottom of the triangle serves as, of course, the foundation. Before you can consider becoming a 50+ athlete, you must have a clean bill of health and a solid baseline of fitness. People often rush

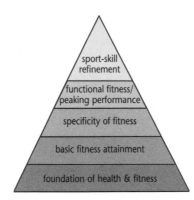

Elements for Top Performance

through this level and pay the price with significant injury or even sudden death. Train to play! Playing your sport to get fit is a mistake.

BASIC FITNESS ATTAINMENT
Any 50+ athlete who wants to avoid injury must have an above-average level of strength, aerobic endurance, flexibility and balance. It's highly recommended that you engage in a basic weight-machine workout using the compound muscles of the body for a minimum of four to six weeks before moving to the next level. Additionally, you should have the ability to exercise moderately/vigorously without any adverse effects. If you rush through this level, you are subject to injury.

SPECIFICITY OF FITNESS   This level focuses on the specific physiologic aspects required for your specific sport. You'll perform isolated exercises with

such things as free weights and exercise bands, as well as moves associated with your sport. You should spend two to six weeks at this level, taking care not to overtrain. Train smart, not hard.

FUNCTIONAL FITNESS/PEAKING PERFORMANCE   The training routines contained within this book are aimed at peaking 50+ athletes' fitness skills to separate them from those who are simply training. At this level, the activities that you perform should foster sport-specific skills. Every exercise move should be associated with your sport. Exercises in this level can parallel your participation in your season.

SPORT-SKILL REFINEMENT   At this peak level of performance, minor tweaks in techniques can shave seconds off your time or strokes off your score. When training at this level, a knowledgeable coach in biomechanics and techniques is critical. Many amateur athletes are willing to spend enormous amounts of money on equipment without wanting to spend the time improving their fitness skills.

before you begin

Exercise slogans have changed throughout the years. You might remember "no pain, no gain" from the 1960s. In the 1990s, it became "no mild discomfort, no gain." Today the slogan isn't quite as catchy but it means well: "Every little bit helps but if you can do it more often and longer but not necessarily harder, you can gain great results."

Finding the correct exercise prescription that is right for you depends upon your goals and your health history. What's moderate for one person may be vigorous for another; what's easy for someone may be hard for someone else. But any pain that exceeds mild soreness means you're overdoing it and risking injury.

Some older athletes suffer from the "forever 21"complex, refusing to accept that they cannot still train like they did when they were 21. No one would have thought that Bob, 51, former track star and vintage athlete, would die of a sudden heart attack while out for his training run. Unfortunately, it can happen to anyone.

Many older athletes can work out intensely because their ability to exercise hasn't diminished with age, but their potential to get hurt while exercising has increased. Being over 50 is no reason to stop working out, however. You need to exercise smart, not hard, to reduce your risk of injury. For this reason, consult with your doctor before engaging in any new kind of physical activity.

Tell your health professional about your fitness goals and allow him or her to determine how extensive the medical assessment should be. The demands of your activity will often determine how extensive the evaluation will be. Thus, if you plan to participate in triathlons, your medical exam should be more comprehensive than someone who wants to pick up golf.

Determining Your Fitness Level

Once you've gotten the all clear, determine your fitness category using the box on page 14.

Regardless of your fitness level, always keep safety in mind. The chosen exercise should also work the targeted muscle, be biomechanically correct, and be compatible with your program goal. Most importantly, the benefits of any

14

Which fitness level best (and most honestly) describes you?

1. **Physically elite:** You train regularly and vigorously to participate and compete in senior sports.

2. **Physically fit:** You exercise at least twice a week for health enjoyment and well-being. You can perform all advanced activities of daily living.

3. **Physically independent:** You are active and functionally independent, but may have diminished levels of balance, coordination, strength and flexibility. You can participate in low–physical demand activities such as walking and golf.

4. **Physically frail:** You can perform basic activities of daily living that are only slightly demanding (for instance, bathing, dressing, toileting).

5. **Physically dependent:** You have significant difficulty performing basic activities of daily living and need home health care or institutional care.

6. **Totally disabled:** You are unable to perform basic activities of daily living and require total assistance from professional staff.

If you answered 1, 2 or 3, you are the ideal candidate for the *Total Sports Conditioning for Athletes 50+* programs. If you answered 4, 5 or 6, consult your medical doctor and ask what steps you can take to become fitter. A few visits to a trained physical therapist can make a big difference. Then look at my other books (*Stretching for 50+* and *Weights for 50+*) and ask your therapist to select the exercises that will move you in the right direction. Remember, what you do today will determine how you age tomorrow.

exercise should outweigh the risks. Any exercise that has made it into your routine should give you maximum return on your investment.

Setting Goals

To improve performance, you need a goal to give you direction. Consider these questions:

Specific—what are you trying to accomplish?

Measurable—how many/how fast?

Action—what do you need to do to make your goal happen?

Realistic—can it be achieved given your skill/health set?

Timely—can it be accomplished given the time you have available?

Goals can be measured in various ways:

• Will you be satisfied if you just accomplish the task (e.g., complete a 10K race)?

• Will you be satisfied if you're in the top 5% of your age group?

• Will you be satisfied if you beat your personal best?

• Will you be satisfied simply with the "process" of training?

None of the above is better than another.

Once you've decided upon a goal, you can design a program.

Tools of the Trade

Although no gym requirement is required to successfully per-

form the programs in this book, you will benefit from a few pieces of equipment that can be purchased from sporting goods stores. Consider them as important as comfortable clothing and a good pair of appropriate workout shoes.

Dumbbells, or free weights, are used to develop muscular strength. If possible, purchase a set of weights that allows you to add and subtract the load. These weights should have secure locking devices that prevent the weight plates from slipping off. Always check the weights before use to avoid this incident. **Elastic bands or tubing** provide resistance and can often replace dumbbells. A **weight vest** can be worn to increase the load for body-weight moves such as push-ups and lunges.

Stability or balance balls help develop the core by challenging your balance. Be sure the size of the ball is suitable for your height. Your legs should form a 90-degree angle when you sit on the ball and place your feet flat on the floor. **Medicine balls** are used to improve explosive power. Take care to prevent injuries or getting hit or knocked over by the ball.

A **yoga mat** helps provide cushioning and a non-slippery surface for performing certain ab exercises and stretches.

doing it right

It's an unfortunate reality: Older athletes are more likely to injure themselves than younger athletes doing the same activity. In addition, 60 percent of vintage athletes who begin an exercise program suffer an athletic injury within the first six weeks. The good news is that approximately 85 percent of sports injuries in the 50-plus group are overuse injuries and respond well to conservative treatment.

Most of the chronic conditions seen in older athletes are the result of misuse (poor body mechanics) and disuse (inactivity and then doing too much). Generally, younger athletes can heal and rehabilitate much faster and more efficiently than a 50-plus body. Older athletes are much like vintage automobiles: if well maintained and treated with tender loving care, they can run on and on. However, if they're misused or abused, they'll break down long before the warranty expires. If you don't want to have a total overhaul, be careful when you exercise and understand your limits.

At the present time very little is known about how hard middle-aged athletes should push themselves. No one yet knows what the ideal dose is to produce the ideal response, so the most prudent advice is: Train, don't strain!

You should only exercise to a point that you can tolerate comfortably. Exercise should not, and does not, have to be painful. Be aware of your capabilities and exercise within your limitations. If you exercise too strenuously, you may be setting yourself up for injury.

The areas athletes most frequently injure are the joints of the back, shoulder, knee, elbow and ankle. Soft tissue injuries to tendons and ligaments, which include sprains, rotator cuff tendonitis, plantar fasciitis and Achilles tendonitis, are the bane of many vintage athletes. Repeated running and jumping is often too much for the meniscus (the shock absorber) of the knee. Repetitive motions like swimming and throwing a baseball often take a toll on the rotator cuff of the shoulder.

As you may well know, prevention is cheaper than treatment. Just following these 12 simple guidelines can prevent many injuries.

1. **Warm up before starting**. Increase the blood flow to the muscles to increase flexibility. Generally, a good warm-up is performing the moves of your sport gently prior to your actual workout.

2. **Stretch properly.** The best time to stretch is when the muscles are warm, usually after a workout. Avoid stretching ballistically, or bouncing, because it actually causes the stretched muscle to contract and shorten, which may induce strain or micro-tears of the muscle fibers. For excellent stretches for the vintage athlete, please check out my other book, *Stretching for 50+* (Ulysses Press).

3. **Get in shape to play.** Too many weekend warriors think that just going out to play will get them in shape to compete. Nothing is farther from the truth. Design your workout to match the demands of your

sport. Proper strength training around a joint will help to stabilize and protect it from further damage.

4. **Engage proper body mechanics.** Playing tennis with a bad racquet, running with poor form, and cycling with poor body mechanics can all lead to injuries. Make sure that you're not playing in worn-out shoes, which can lead to additional problems. Do warm-up motions slowly. Do not overextend or "lock out" any joints. Protect your back and stabilize your low back. Keep your shoulders away from your ears.

5. **Avoid overtraining.** Overtraining is a major concern for the highly active fitness participant and occurs as a result of dramatically increasing training periods with high-volume or high-intensity workouts without adequate rest. The consequences can be both psychological and physiological manifestations. Common signs of overtraining include feeling more pain, less desire to train, loss of appetite, difficulty concentrating and emotional instability.

6. **Obtain your ideal weight.** For every pound of weight loss, there is a four-pound reduction in load placed upon your joints with each step. A pound of weight loss would mean 4,800 pounds less load

placed on the knee for every mile walked. Less weight = less pressure = less knee pain.

7. **Choose the right sport for you.** Your sport should match both your body type and your personality. If the sport doesn't feel right or you're getting hurt too often, it might not be the correct fit for you. If you're very social, you'd do best in team sports, golf, tennis or dancing; if you prefer to be alone, running or swimming would be ideal for you.

8. **Cross-train.** Mixing up activities/sports on alternate days is a great way to avoid burnout and overtraining.

9. **Listen to your body.** If something hurts or doesn't feel right, back off and rest. Put off exercise for any of the following reasons:

- Your muscle aches from a viral infection.
- Your blood pressure systolic is greater than 150 at rest and your diastolic exceeds 100 at rest, or your heart rate is greater than 110 at rest.
- A joint is red, swollen, warm or painful.
- You are having chest pains, heart flutters or any other signs of a stroke or heart attack (this would be a good time to call 911).
- Your limbs are swollen.
- Breathing is difficult.

In addition, don't use perspiration as an indication of how good (or bad) your workout is: we all perspire at different rates and in different amounts.

10. **Take care of yourself.** Seek prompt medical care for injuries. The sooner you see a doctor, the quicker you'll return to the field. In addition, if acute injuries are treated properly and quickly, there's less chance it will turn into a chronic problem. Locate a good sports medicine doctor and/or physical therapist who can assist you in getting back into form.

11. **Learn the difference between good pain and bad pain.** Too many athletes push themselves too hard. There are four stages of training: comfort, hurt, pain and agony. Each person has his or her own threshold for pain but the recommendation is still to train, don't strain. Chronic, long-standing pain is bad. Joint pain is generally bad.

12. **Know your environment.** Training in the heat presents a totally different set of issues than training in the cold. Wear layers when training in the cold. Since it's easy to get sick or even die when training incorrectly in the heat, doing so requires a bit more caution. The following tips can prevent some major health problems:

- The thirst mechanism is not as alert in older athletes as in younger folks. Drink fluids frequently—water is an excellent source. Power drinks are not needed for most athletes.
- Avoid salt tablets and drinks with high concentration of salt and sugar.
- Be alert to heat indexes that take into consideration, temperature, wind speed, and humidity.
- Train in the shade, not in the sun. Plan your workouts at the coolest time of the day and don't forget to protect your skin.
- Arrive a few days ahead of an event to acclimatize yourself to the heat and humidity. While on vacation, adjust your workouts accordingly.
- Stay cool. Wear hats that allow ventilation and avoid clothing and socks that lock in heat.
- Protect your feet with socks that absorb sweat.

Other Common Concerns

This section discusses common concerns that arise during and after exercise.

Breathing

Breathing is an automatic, unconscious action, yet some of us hold our breath when exerting ourselves. The most important thing about breathing is not to concentrate on any particular "way" to breathe, but to do so comfortably and freely. If you find yourself holding your breath, count out loud or talk to your partner while doing the exercise.

Rest

If you learn to listen to your body and heed what it says, your body will tell you when and how long to rest. While the average person rests far too much, you as an athlete are often afraid to rest in fear of deconditioning. This is why cross-training is an excellent way to stay active yet not overdo it.

When lifting weights, you should allow a day for the body to rebuild and recover. As an athlete, you're probably very motivated and might want to lift daily. A method you can try is to do upper body work one day and lower body the next. Another option is to do the push/pull method (basically every exercise that requires pushing: bench press, push-ups) one day and then only do pulling exercises (such as bicep curls and lat pulls) the next.

The amount of rest between sets will depend on your objectives and your fitness level. If you're training for strength and size, you'll be lifting heavier weights and will require more rest between sets to recover as well as longer time off between workouts to rebuild and recover. However, if you're training for fitness and muscular endurance, try to limit the rest time between sets. Keep in mind that it's the time spent exercising in the gym that makes you fit, not the time spent in the gym. Standing around talking between sets doesn't do much for fitness.

Don't squeeze a week's worth of exercise into one day—spread your exercise sessions evenly throughout the week and make sure you alternate "hard" and "easy" days.

After intense exercise, never come to an immediate rest. Instead, continue with low-intensity exercise such as walking to encourage proper return of blood to the heart, preventing any blood-pooling effect that may occur in the lower extremities. Keep your head above heart level until you've cooled down, and move slowly between positions of lying down, sitting or standing.

Muscular issues

Muscle cramps can be brought on by inadequate blood flow, lack of essential electrolytes, fluids or general muscle fatigue. To help eliminate cramping, you should first stretch the muscles that are involved. For example, cramps of the calf are common: to eliminate these, gently pull your toes back towards you and hold this position. Next, to increase blood flow to the area, try rubbing the muscle.

Muscle soreness may be expected after beginning an exercise program following a long period of inactivity. During exercise, the muscle and connective tissue may be minutely torn, causing spasms and fluid retention. Muscle spasms can irritate nerve endings, thus causing pain. To help prevent soreness, warm up and stretch properly, progress slowly in your exercise program, and cool down after each exercise section. If muscle soreness should occur, mild stretching and a low-intensity activity such as walking can help relieve discomfort. If you experience cramps on a regular basis, consult your doctor; there could be other issues contributing to your cramps.

Fluid Intake

In order for the body to carry out its normal physiological processes, the body needs, among many other things, water. To exercise safely, you should consume water before, during and after exercise to ensure that water you have lost through sweat is replenished. This is especially important on warm and humid days. For most people, regular water is all that's needed. A simple test to see if you are hydrated enough is to check the color of your urine. Light, pale yellow urine is what you want to see. If it's very dark, try increasing your intake of water. Additionally, if you're a long-distance runner, weigh yourself before and after your run. If you are dropping a lot of weight on the run, increase your fluid intake.

The Whole Package

A total fitness program involves muscular strength and endurance, flexibility, balance, coordination and cardiovascular endurance. The new recommendations from the Centers for Disease Control (CDC) and American College of Sports Medicine (ACSM) suggest that people simply engage in any physical activity, regardless of Target Heart Rate (THR), most days of the week. More and more research suggests that mild to moderate physical activity is all that is needed to be healthy.

ing, bicycling, swimming and cross-country skiing.

Strength training may include the use of free weights, sandbags, pulleys, elastic bands or any other device that is safe and provides adequate resistance.

Cool-down following exercise is as valuable as a proper warm-up. Too many athletes skip this portion of the routine because they consider it a waste of time, but this is the ideal time to perform static stretches. If you have chronic issues, focus on those areas. Stretching and slow walking for 5 to 15 minutes allow the body to recover from exercise and maintain the body's suppleness, helping to keep you injury free.

Top off your program by drinking plenty of water as well as checking your heart rate before, during and after each exercise session. Don't overestimate your body's capacity to exercise but don't underestimate it, either. Your body is designed for movement, but let it adapt slowly and gradually. By training smart, you'll not only improve your game, you'll become stronger and healthier while reducing injuries. In the game of life, the person who comes in last wins!

Warming up and stretching are essential parts of every exercise session, and not just on cold days. The purpose of the warm-up (5 to 15 minutes) is to prepare the body for exercise. This is accomplished by beginning the exercise session at a very low level of intensity and gradually making it more vigorous. By slowly increasing your activity, you are allowing the blood to flow into the muscles and thus raising muscular temperature. As the temperature increases, the muscles and connective tissue become more pliable and less susceptible to injury.

The aerobic portion of the workout should consist of activities that use large-muscle groups (e.g., legs) continuously for a minimum of 20 minutes. Examples of aerobic activities include brisk walk-

part 2:
the
programs

how to use this book

This section offers thirteen sport-specific programs ranging from baseball to tennis, all designed for vintage athletes. Pick the program that best matches your preferred sport or activity and then determine the level (untrained/off-season, trained/in-season) you should start at. Where you start and the pace you progress at has more to do with your health and wellness than your age.

These programs are complete workouts that will complement your sport-specific training. They start with warm-ups, continue with functional exercises specific to your sport, and end with essential cool-downs. Therefore, once you've chosen your program, follow the progression that's laid out, performing all the moves that your body allows. Ideally, you'd train three to five times a week. If you notice an increase in pain, ease up on the sets/reps/intensity until you find the correct dose. If you experience pain in a joint, stop that

exercise. If post-exercise discomfort is significant two hours post-workout, back off.

Moving from one level to the next is a rather subjective decision. However, as an athlete you should be familiar with the "feel" of exercise, thus when you feel that the existing level is too easy, then move up to the next level. Some people will choose to perform a challenging workout one day and then back off to the lower level for the next workout. Some other things to consider: how does your heart rate respond to the new workout? Can you

still carry on a conversation while training? Do you feel increased discomfort or increased post-exercise pain?

The basic premise of *Total Sports Conditioning for 50+* is to train wisely for your game. The key is specificity of training—performing motions that provide a real carryover benefit to the application you are pursuing, whether it's running, tennis or swimming. In other words, to be a better tennis player, you don't play golf. The exercises in this book are gentle on joints, yet they're functional and challenging for the vintage athlete.

All the exercises included in the programs are designed to improve your ability to participate fully in the recreational pursuits that make your life complete while maintaining an element of fun. Sports require a variety of movements and you'll find them here, from lower-body work (walking, jogging, sprinting, cutting, jumping) to upper-body moves (throwing, catching, swinging). Remember, when performing any exercise, focus on proper execution—not speed or number of repetitions.

Most sports and recreational activities require you to carry or move your body through space. Learning to move your body easily and correctly will foster better performance. *Free-form exercises* (e.g., Pilates push-up, side-to-side hops) employ your body weight as the tool to improve muscular strength and endurance. They engage the complete body unit and are superior to machines because you're responsible for executing the movement with proper form while fostering core strength. Additionally, these exercises engage both the major and minor muscle groups of the body.

Compound exercises (e.g., lunge with horizontal press, side lunge with upright row) engage the total body by doing multiple moves. For example, compound exercises will incorporate leg moves while simultaneously performing upper body strength-training activities.

The *big ball* exercises foster greater core strength and awareness of the midsection while performing compound motions. The midsection, or "abs," is commonly called the core. The core, however, is not just the muscles of the abdominal area but also the superficial muscles of the lower back as well as the deep-lying muscles of the pelvic complex. The core is often considered the "powerhouse" of the body with regard to sports performance, and a solid core will improve performance and posture. Core stability is critical in the prevention of lower back problems.

The *medicine ball* exercises yield greater power and reaction time in the chest and shoulder region. They're designed to improve power in the upper body, which is useful in racquet sports, baseball and softball.

Balance is a major component of most sports. The *balance exercises* enhance static and dynamic balance, both of which are critical for functional activities, fall prevention and sports fitness. The static moves improve ankle stabilization and should be performed with ease before progressing to the dynamic moves. The dynamic balance exercises are suitable only for advanced individuals with excellent balance and no joint issues. Don't do these exercises if you have a history of falling. Make sure the area around you is safe and secure.

The *agility and speed exercises* are very challenging to the cardiovascular system and joints. They will facilitate your performance in most sports, including basketball and tennis, by enhancing footwork and reducing soft tissue injuries such as strains and sprains. Since these are very advanced moves, use caution before engaging in them and avoid them altogether if you have any orthopedic issues, such as arthritis of the hip/knee/ankle, lower back issues,

DESIGNING FUNCTIONAL PROGRAMS

1. Understand the demands and skills of your sport.
2. Understand the physical requirements of your sport, be they strength, flexibility, agility, speed, quickness, and/or coordination, then incorporate those aspects into your routine.
3. Understand if your sport relies on raw athletic traits or on sport precision. Find a coach that understands the finer aspects of your sport and matches your personality.
4. Design a training routine that matches your physical abilities and limitations as well as time and equipment.

and hip or knee replacements. It is always prudent to consult your physical therapist or medical doctor if you have some orthopedic issues When you do take on these drills, be sure you are adequately trained and warmed up before performing them.

Getting Ready for the Game

When embarking on your conditioning program, consider whether you plan to compete or have just finished the event. The training intensity will depend to a large extent on what your objective is as well as when the event is. The variable of time to a very large extent determines how hard and how long you need to train. Keep in mind that the volume of your workout can influence your risk of injury. A person can train very hard for a short period of time or train at a lesser intensity for a longer period time and attain similar results. A general rule of thumb is that harder workouts put the person at a greater risk of injury. You should design both on- and off-season programs (as shown in the sports programs). A commitment to year-round sensible training is one reason why today's athletes are faster, stronger and better than athletes of yore.

YEAR-ROUND TRAINING SCHEDULE

Level 1: Foundational Skills

Build your foundation by focusing on:

- Posture
- Range of motion
- Balance
- Establishing a baseline of muscular strength and endurance
- Establishing a baseline of cardiovascular fitness and respiratory reserve
- Improving functional skills and activities of daily living

Level 2: Fitness Skills

Build your fitness by focusing on:

- Proper execution and form
- Not increasing pain or symptoms
- Increasing/maintaining cardiovascular fitness
- Increasing/maintaining muscular strength and endurance
- Increasing/maintaining balance
- Increasing/maintaining coordination
- Increasing/maintaining flexibility

Level 3: Competition Skills

If your activity desires this level of sports conditioning, this is the time to explore periodization, engage in interval training and incorporate more sports agility drills and sport-specific skills. At this stage you will be ramping up the volume and intensity.

First, pick an event you wish to do your best in and then design a training routine backwards from there. For example, let's say you want to compete in an open-water swim on May 15. Here's what your training schedule would look like:

January–February: Engage in relaxed conditioning swims and aerobic conditioning biking. Perform an exercise program that fosters the strength needed for your stroke, and corrective exercises (such as rotator cuff exercises) that will prevent injury.

March–April: Increase training intensity. Seek a coach to refine your swim strokes and increase muscle conditioning for your event.

May 1–May 15: Consider tapering off and consider your diet, carbo-loading if appropriate, for your event. Perform mental practice for your event: imagine what the water will feel like, what the field of competitors will look like, how you will handle the pre-race jitters.

Notice that we've incorporated periodization into the training program. You should do the same. Three to six months before your season, you should focus on levels 1 and 2 (refer to "Year-round Training Schedule" box) and develop a baseline of fitness. By spending more time in this phase, you will better equip yourself for the physical demands of your event. This is foundation time, and your body is the temple. No great temple was ever built on a shaky foundation.

One to two months prior to the start of your season, move

to Level 3. This would also be a good time to check your equipment and maybe have a specialist in your sport check your form and body mechanics. Swimmers, for example, can shave time off their event if they can tweak their form just slightly. Do everything you can to avoid injury—unfortunately, this is when most people get hurt because they're trying to make up for inadequate foundation time. Overtraining now can definitely ruin your season.

Note that if your sport has a long season and you want to compete/participate in several events, you'll need to design a program that will allow you to peak, then taper off, then peak again for the grand finale of the season. Also, it's wise to change your program every three months to challenge the muscles in a different manner and to prevent boredom.

Once your season ends, return to Level 1. Don't lie on the couch until the season rolls around again. Plan now to take all the steps necessary to keep you tuned up for next season and avoid de-conditioning. Maybe now would be a good time to attend clinics and improve skills, or see a physical therapist to rehabilitate chronic injuries. If you're a dual-sport person, you'll want to start training for your next sport.

Avoiding the Dreaded Plateau

A neophyte to exercise will make improvements quite drastically in a reasonably short period of time. This is because the body is not acquainted to the demands of exercise and adapts to those stresses quickly. If you've been training for a while (usually three to six months), however, you might feel like you've stopped improving. Basically, your training routine has reached its saturation point and your body is no longer being challenged. This is called a plateau. Don't get discouraged—there are several things you can do to get your body on track.

- Rest allows your body to recuperate. For most people, a two- to three-week period is all they need. Periodization techniques may be incorporated to train the body in a different cycle.

- Change your program and cross-train. If you play tennis, try cycling instead to keep you fit but give your mind and body a break.

- The literature suggests that for ongoing improvements the body should experience a two- to five-percent challenge each week.

There are numerous ways to overload the body—think of FIT:

F—Increase the **frequency** of the workout.

I—Increase the **intensity** of the workout within reason.

T—Increase the **time** of the interval (e.g., more reps per set), or decrease the rest period between intervals.

Keep in mind, however, that much of the literature on training is based on college-age athletes and that too much of an overload can cause an injury. Some trainers contend that a person can continually make improvements, but numerous factors contradict that theory. At some point you *will* max out your potential—no one can continue to always and forever improve. It's at this point that you don't get tempted to take "magic potions" to improve performance. Push yourself to reach realistic goals based upon your age and physiologic make-up and enjoy yourself while you're doing it. Train smart, not hard, to avoid sitting on the injured reserve bench. A quality workout is always better than a large-quantity workout.

BASEBALL/SOFTBALL

Baseball and softball performance can be greatly enhanced by the proper use of conditioning. In addition, a combination of weight training, stretching and functional fitness will prevent injuries and improve your ability. Each position requires a different set of skills and conditioning routines. Pitchers *need cardiovascular fitness, lower body strength and endurance* along with muscular endurance and proper flexibility of the shoulders. Catchers *require explosive leg strength with good flexibility, as well as hand and wrist strength and a solid core.* Outfielders *also need strong legs along with solid upper body strength.* Infielders *need good hand-eye coordination and agility.*

Pre-season training should start four to six weeks before the season starts. Training should be done three days a week with one day of rest between workouts. The in-season focus should be on your sports training; gym-time intensity can be downsized to two days a week if you are playing a lot.

			Untrained/ Off season	Trained/ In season
W	p. 54	forward lunge with rotator cuff	1 x 5	2 x 10–15
	p. 55	arm swing with neck turn	1 x 5	2 x 10–15
	p. 57	knee to chest	1 x 5	2 x 10–15
	p. 56	heel/toe raise	1 x 5	2 x 10–15
C	p. 58	lunge with vertical press	1 x 5	2 x 10–15
	p. 60	side lunge with upright row	1 x 5	2 x 10–15
	p. 64	squat with dumbbell	1 x 5	2 x 10–15
	p. 65	half-squat with lateral/frontal raise	1 x 5	2 x 10–15
	p. 70	pilates push-up	1 x 5	2 x 10–15
	p. 73	inverted pull-up	1 x 5	2 x 10–15
	p. 75	reverse fly	1 x 5	2 x 10–15
	p. 77	military press on ball	1 x 5	2 x 10–15
CR	p. 82	swimming	1 x 5	2 x 10–15
	p. 86	plank	1 x 15 sec. hold	2 x 30–60 sec. hold
	p. 88	twist with band	1 x 5	2 x 10–15

BASEBALL/SOFTBALL

			Untrained/ Off season	Trained/ In season
CR		p. 89 downward chopping	1 x 5	2 x 10–15
		p. 90 upward chopping	1 x 5	2 x 10–15
B		p. 92 stork stand	1 x 10–30 sec. hold	2 x 30–60 sec. hold
A		p. 99 speed play	1 x 10–12	1 x 15–20
		p. 102 circle jumps	1 x 10–30	2 x 30–60
		p. 103 side-to-side hops	1 x 10–30	2 x 30–60
		p. 107 superball bounce	1 x 5	2 x 10–15
T		p. 110 under-arm toss	1 x 5	2 x 10–15
		p. 111 throwing motion with band	1 x 5	2 x 10–15
F		p. 114 double wood chop	1 x 30 sec. hold	2 x 30–60 sec. hold
		p. 116 the zipper	1 x 30 sec. hold	2 x 30–60 sec. hold
		p. 114 choker	1 x 30 sec. hold	2 x 30–60 sec. hold
		p. 117 palm tree	1 x 30 sec. hold	2 x 30–60 sec. hold
		p. 118 twister	1 x 30 sec. hold	2 x 30–60 sec. hold
		p. 129 wrist stretch standing	1 x 30 sec. hold	2 x 30–60 sec. hold
		p. 127 rear calf stretch	1 x 30 sec. hold	2 x 30–60 sec. hold

W WARM-UP   **C** CONDITIONING   **CR** CORE   **B** BALANCE   **A** AGILITY   **T** TOSS   **F** FLEXIBILITY

BASKETBALL

Basketball players need explosiveness along with general fitness. Your program should foster agility, core stability, muscular endurance and excellent cardiovascular fitness. Flexibility is important for injury prevention. Cross-training is always a good idea to prevent you from beating up your body on the court.

Pre-season training should start four to six weeks before the season starts. Training should be done three days a week with one day of rest between workouts. Create a program that works out your entire body and corrects muscle imbalances. The in-season focus should be on your sports training; gym-time intensity can be downsized to two days a week if you are playing a lot.

			Untrained/ Off season	Trained/ In season
W	p. 53	side lunge with frontal/lateral raise	1 x 5	2 x 10–15
	p. 54	forward lunge with rotator cuff	1 x 5	2 x 10–15
	p. 56	heel/toe raise	1 x 5	2 x 10–15
C	p. 58	lunge with vertical press	1 x 5	2 x 10–15
	p. 59	lunge with horizontal press	1 x 5	2 x 10–15
	p. 61	bench step-up	1 x 5	2 x 10–15
	p. 64	squat with dumbbell	1 x 5	2 x 10–15
	p. 65	half-squat with lateral/frontal raise	1 x 5	2 x 10–15
	p. 70	pilates push-up	1 x 5	2 x 10–15
	p. 68	wide push-up	1 x 5	2 x 10–15
	p. 75	reverse fly	1 x 5	2 x 10–15
	p. 77	military press on ball	1 x 5	2 x 10–15
CR	p. 78	curl-up	1 x 5	2 x 10–15
	p. 79	diagonal curl-up	1 x 5	2 x 10–15
	p. 80	ball roll-out	1 x 5	2 x 10–15
	p. 84	pelvic lift	1 x 5	2 x 10–15
	p. 86	plank	1 x 15 sec. hold	2 x 30–60 sec. hold

BASKETBALL

			Untrained/ Off season	Trained/ In season
CR		p. 88 twist with dumbbell	1 x 5	2 x 10–15
B		p. 96 forward jump & hold	1 x 10–15	2 x 15–30
		p. 97 lateral jump & hold	1 x 10–15	2 x 15–30
		p. 98 one-leg hop & hold	1 x 10–15	2 x 15–30
A		p. 100 lateral shuffle	1 x 10–30	2 x 30–60
		p. 101 stair jump	1 x 10–30	2 x 30–60
		p. 102 circle jumps	1 x 10–30	2 x 30–60
		p. 104 double-leg hops	1 x 10–30	2 x 30–60
		p. 105 single-leg jumps	1 x 10–30	2 x 30–60
		p. 106 jumping rope	1–3 min.	5–10 min.
		p. 107 superball bounce	1 x 5	2 x 10–15
T		p. 108 bench press & catch	1 x 5	2 x 10–15
		p. 109 military press & catch	1 x 5	2 x 10–15
F		p. 117 palm tree	1 x 30 sec. hold	2 x 30–60 sec. hold
		p. 118 twister	1 x 30 sec. hold	2 x 30–60 sec. hold
		p. 128 ankle circle	30 sec.	30–60 sec.
		p. 124 quad stretch	1 x 30 sec. hold	2 x 30–60 sec. hold
		p. 123 the butterfly	1 x 30 sec. hold	2 x 30–60 sec. hold
		p. 122 inverted figure 4	1 x 30 sec. hold	2 x 30–60 sec. hold
		p. 127 rear calf stretch	1 x 30 sec. hold	2 x 30–60 sec. hold

BASKETBALL

| W | WARM-UP | C | CONDITIONING | CR | CORE | B | BALANCE | A | AGILITY | T | TOSS | F | FLEXIBILITY |

CYCLING

Cycling requires upper leg strength and endurance as well as back endurance and even arm strength. Your specific training program will depend on whether you're a sprinter or an endurance rider. Sprinters need explosive speed and a high anaerobic threshold, whereas endurance riders need the ability to endure long sessions in the saddle. The best way to improve is to train at intensities and distances you plan to compete in.

Pre-season training should start four to six weeks before the season starts. Training should be done three days a week with one day of rest between workouts. Create a program that corrects any muscle imbalances. The in-season focus should be on your sports training; gym-time intensity can be downsized to two days a week if you are riding a lot.

			Untrained/ Off season	Trained/ In season
W	p. 52	knee lift	1 x 30 sec.	2 x 60 sec.
	p. 55	arm swing with neck turn	1 x 5	2 x 10–15
	p. 56	heel/toe raise	1 x 5	2 x 10–15
	p. 57	knee to chest	1 x 5	2 x 10–15
C	p. 61	bench step-up	1 x 5	2 x 10–15
	p. 64	squat with dumbbell	1 x 5	2 x 10–15
	p. 65	half-squat with lateral/frontal raise	1 x 5	2 x 10–15
	p. 70	pilates push-up	1 x 5	2 x 10–15
	p. 67	push-up	1 x 5	2 x 10–15
	p. 68	diamond push-up	1 x 5	2 x 10–15
	p. 75	reverse fly	1 x 5	2 x 10–15
	p. 76	bench press on ball	1 x 5	2 x 10–15
CR	p. 79	diagonal curl-up	1 x 5	2 x 10–15
	p. 86	plank	1 x 15 sec. hold	2 x 30–60 sec. hold
	p. 87	side plank	1 x 15 sec. hold	2 x 30–60 sec. hold

CYCLING

				Untrained/ Off season	Trained/ In season
CR		p. 91	lunge & twist	1 x 5	2 x 10–15
		p. 81	pointer series	1 x 5	2 x 10–15--
B		p. 93	bike ride	1 x for 10–30 sec.	2 x for 30–60 sec.
A		p. 98	one-leg hop & hold	1 x 10–15	2 x 15–30
		p. 101	stair jump	1 x 10–30	2 x 30–60
		p. 99	speed play	1 x 10–12	1 x 15–20
F		p. 124	quad stretch	1 x 30 sec. hold	2 x 30–60 sec. hold
		p. 115	hands behind back	1 x 30 sec. hold	2 x 30–60 sec. hold
		p. 121	roll into a ball	1 x 30 sec. hold	2 x 30–60 sec. hold
		p. 122	inverted figure 4	1 x 30 sec. hold	2 x 30–60 sec. hold
		p. 128	ankle circle	30 sec.	30–60 sec.
		p. 129	wrist stretch standing	1 x 30 sec. hold	2 x 30–60 sec. hold
		p. 127	rear calf stretch	1 x 30 sec. hold	2 x 30–60 sec. hold
		p. 119	cross-leg drop	1 x 30 sec. hold	2 x 30–60 sec. hold

CYCLING

W WARM-UP	**C** CONDITIONING	**CR** CORE	**B** BALANCE	**A** AGILITY	**T** TOSS	**F** FLEXIBILITY

GOLF

Golf is a tough game on the body, requiring twisting of the knees and forceful rotation of the lower back. In addition, golf is an asymmetrical sport, with moves performed repeatedly in one direction. Unfortunately, the worse the golfer, the more the movement is repeated. Another issue presents itself when a cart is used—sitting around allows the body to become tight and therefore unprepared for the next bout of action.

While golf does not require big muscles, it does require power, which is strength combined with speed. The goal of your workout session should be to undo any and all muscle imbalances caused by your game. Then it should focus on the muscles needed for the game and, whenever possible, replicate the speed of movements used while playing. Most teaching pros suggest that the legs, torso and shoulders should become one fluid kinetic chain. Leg stamina and core stability are critical in transferring leg energy through the torso, into the shoulders, down the arms into the club and thus into the movement of the ball.

Flexibility is central in injury prevention. Be careful with those cool morning start times—make sure your body is adequately warmed up before swinging away. Also, since golf is a social game, use your training session to burn those 19th-hole calories!

			Untrained/ Off season	Trained/ In season
W	p. 57	knee to chest	1 x 5	2 x 10–15
	p. 54	forward lunge with rotator cuff	1 x 5	2 x 10–15
	p. 55	arm swing with neck turn	1 x 5	2 x 10–15
C	p. 61	bench step-up	1 x 5	2 x 10–15
	p. 62	bench side-step	1 x 5	2 x 10–15
	p. 65	half-squat with lateral/frontal raise	1 x 5	2 x 10–15
	p. 75	reverse fly	1 x 5	2 x 10–15
	p. 73	inverted pull-up	1 x 5	2 x 10–15
CR	p. 78	curl-up	1 x 5	2 x 10–15
	p. 79	diagonal curl-up	1 x 5	2 x 10–15
	p. 81	pointer series	1 x 5	2 x 10–15
	p. 83	back extension over ball	1 x 5	2 x 10–15

GOLF

			Untrained/ Off season	Trained/ In season
CR	p. 86	plank	1 x 15 sec. hold	2 x 30–60 sec. hold
	p. 87	side plank	1 x 15 sec. hold	2 x 30–60 sec. hold
	p. 88	twist with band	1 x 5	2 x 10–15
	p. 89	downward chopping	1 x 5	2 x 10–15
	p. 90	upward chopping	1 x 5	2 x 10–15
	p. 91	lunge & twist	1 x 5	2 x 10–15
	p. 63	double-leg lift	1 x 5	2 x 10–15
B	p. 92	stork stand	1 x 10–30 sec. hold	2 x 30–60 sec. hold
	p. 94	heel-toe stand	1 x 30 sec.	1 x 60 sec.
F	p. 113	double wood chop	1 x 30 sec. hold	2 x 30–60 sec. hold
	p. 114	choker	1 x 30 sec. hold	2 x 30–60 sec. hold
	p. 118	twister	1 x 30 sec. hold	2 x 30–60 sec. hold
	p. 128	ankle circle	30 sec.	30–60 sec.
	p. 129	wrist stretch standing	1 x 30 sec. hold	2 x 30–60 sec. hold
	p. 130	mad cat	1 x 30 sec. hold	2 x 30–60 sec. hold
	p. 127	rear calf stretch	1 x 30 sec. hold	2 x 30–60 sec. hold

GOLF

W WARM-UP   **C** CONDITIONING   **CR** CORE   **B** BALANCE   **A** AGILITY   **T** TOSS   **F** FLEXIBILITY

HOCKEY

Hockey is an intense sport. A team doctor for a professional hockey team said he had never met a group of athletes who could endure more pain than hockey players. To take command of the ice, you need good muscular endurance in the legs, a strong lower back and solid upper body strength. A proper stretching routine is critical for minimizing down time off the ice. Additionally, a proper warm-up is necessary to get ready to play.

Pre-season training should start four to six weeks before the season starts. Training should be done three days a week with one day of rest between workouts. Create a program that corrects any muscle imbalances. The in-season focus should be on your sports training; gym-time intensity can be downsized to two days a week if you are playing a lot.

			Untrained/ Off season	Trained/ In season
W	p. 55	arm swing with neck turn	1 x 5	2 x 10–15
	p. 52	knee lift	1 x 30 sec.	2 x 60 sec.
	p. 57	knee to chest	1 x 5	2 x 10–15
	p. 56	heel/toe raise	1 x 5	2 x 10–15
C	p. 58	lunge with vertical press	1 x 5	2 x 10–15
	p. 59	lunge with horizontal press	1 x 5	2 x 10–15
	p. 66	double-leg thrust with push-up	1 x 5	2 x 10–15
	p. 68	wide push-up	1 x 5	2 x 10–15
	p. 68	clapping push-up	1 x 5	2 x 10–15
	p. 68	diamond push-up	1 x 5	2 x 10–15
	p. 71	chair dip	1 x 5	2 x 10–15
	p. 72	pull-up	1 x 5	2 x 10–15
	p. 74	chin-up	1 x 5	2 x 10–15
	p. 76	bench press on ball	1 x 5	2 x 10–15
	p. 77	military press on ball	1 x 5	2 x 10–15

HOCKEY

HOCKEY

			Untrained/ Off season	Trained/ In season
CR		p. 81 pointer series	1 x 5	2 x 10–15
		p. 83 back extension over ball	1 x 5	2 x 10–15
		p. 63 double-leg lift	1 x 5	2 x 10–15
		p. 86 plank	1 x 15 sec. hold	2 x 30–60 sec. hold
		p. 87 side plank	1 x 15 sec. hold	2 x 30–60 sec. hold
		p. 88 twist with band	1 x 5	2 x 10–15
		p. 91 lunge & twist	1 x 5	2 x 10–15
A		p. 99 speed play	1 x 10–12	1 x 15–20
		p. 103 side-to-side hops	1 x 10–30	2 x 30–60
		p. 104 double-leg hops	1 x 10–30	2 x 30–60
		p. 102 circle jumps	1 x 10–30	2 x 30–60
T		p. 108 bench press & catch	1 x 5	2 x 10–15
		p. 112 medicine ball throw	1 x 5	2 x 10–15
		p. 109 military press & catch	1 x 5	2 x 10–15
F		p. 116 the zipper	1 x 30 sec. hold	2 x 30–60 sec. hold
		p. 115 hands behind back	1 x 30 sec. hold	2 x 30–60 sec. hold
		p. 124 quad stretch	1 x 30 sec. hold	2 x 30–60 sec. hold
		p. 128 ankle circle	30 sec.	30–60 sec.
		p. 127 rear calf stretch	1 x 30 sec. hold	2 x 30–60 sec. hold

HOCKEY

W WARM-UP   **C** CONDITIONING   **CR** CORE   **B** BALANCE   **A** AGILITY   **T** TOSS   **F** FLEXIBILITY

ROWING

Rowing is primarily an endurance sport. However, power is needed for starts, pulling away and strong finishes. Most crew athletes have stronger pulling muscles than pushing muscles, which contribute to muscle imbalances. Although most of the sport's conditioning takes place in the boat, your land-based program should focus on trying to correct those imbalances.

Pre-season training should start four to six weeks before the season starts. Training should be done three days a week with one day of rest between workouts. Create a program that corrects any muscle imbalances. The in-season focus should be on your sports training; gym-time intensity can be downsized to two days a week if you are playing a lot.

			Untrained/ Off season	Trained/ In season
W	p. 52	knee lift	1 x 30 sec.	2 x 60 sec.
	p. 54	forward lunge with rotator cuff	1 x 5	2 x 10–15
	p. 55	arm swing with neck turn	1 x 5	2 x 10–15
C	p.59	lunge with horizontal press	1 x 5	2 x 10–15
	p. 60	side lunge with upright row	1 x 5	2 x 10–15
	p. 65	half-squat with lateral/frontal raise	1 x 5	2 x 10–15
	p. 66	double-leg thrust with push-up	1 x 5	2 x 10–15
	p. 72	pull-up	1 x 5	2 x 10–15
	p. 74	chin-up	1 x 5	2 x 10–15
	p. 71	dip	1 x 5	2 x 10–15
	p. 75	reverse fly	1 x 5	2 x 10–15
CR	p. 80	ball roll-out	1 x 5	2 x 10–15
	p. 81	pointer series	1 x 5	2 x 10–15
	p. 82	swimming	1 x 5	2 x 10–15
	p. 85	pelvic lift with leg extension	1 x 5	2 x 10–15

ROWING

F			Untrained/ Off season	Trained/ In season
	p. 115	hands behind back	1 x 30 sec. hold	2 x 30–60 sec. hold
	p. 117	palm tree	1 x 30 sec. hold	2 x 30–60 sec. hold
	p. 130	mad cat	1 x 30 sec. hold	2 x 30–60 sec. hold
	p. 128	ankle circle	30 sec.	30–60 sec.
	p. 120	double-leg stretch	1 x 30 sec. hold	2 x 30–60 sec. hold
	p. 129	wrist stretch standing	1 x 30 sec. hold	2 x 30–60 sec. hold
	p. 122	inverted figure 4	1 x 30 sec. hold	2 x 30–60 sec. hold
	p. 127	rear calf stretch	1 x 30 sec. hold	2 x 30–60 sec. hold

| W | WARM-UP | C | CONDITIONING | CR | CORE | B | BALANCE | A | AGILITY | T | TOSS | F | FLEXIBILITY |

ROWING

RUNNING/JOGGING

Most runners and joggers have well-developed lower extremities but a virtually nonexistent upper body. Runners and joggers can use fitness routines to balance the body and strengthen the muscles not addressed in running. Depending on whether you're a distance runner or a sprinter, your routine will be different. Runners really need to train smart, not hard. Remember to stretch what is tight and strengthen what is weak. Cross-training is also a good idea since too much time on the road often leads to injuries.

Pre-season training should start four to six weeks before the season starts. Training should be done three days a week with one day of rest between workouts. Create a program that corrects any muscle imbalances. The in-season focus should be on your sports training; gym-time intensity can be downsized to two days a week if you are running a lot. Rest is your friend!!

			Untrained/ Off season	Trained/ In season
W	p. 55	arm swing with neck turn	1 x 5	2 x 10–15
	p. 56	heel/toe raise	1 x 5	2 x 10–15
	p. 57	knee to chest	1 x 5	2 x 10–15
C	p. 59	lunge with horizontal press	1 x 5	2 x 10–15
	p. 61	bench step-up	1 x 5	2 x 10–15
	p. 62	bench side-step	1 x 5	2 x 10–15
	p. 60	side lunge with upright row	1 x 5	2 x 10–15
	p. 70	pilates push-up	1 x 5	2 x 10–15
	p. 73	inverted pull-up	1 x 5	2 x 10–15
	p. 75	reverse fly	1 x 5	2 x 10–15
	p. 71	dip	1 x 5	2 x 10–15
CR	p. 78	curl-up	1 x 5	2 x 10–15
	p. 79	diagonal curl-up	1 x 5	2 x 10–15
	p. 86	plank	1 x 15 sec. hold	2 x 30–60 sec. hold
	p. 91	lunge & twist	1 x 5	2 x 10–15

RUNNING/JOGGING

		Untrained/ Off season	Trained/ In season
p. 103	side-to-side hops	1 x 10–30	2 x 30–60
p. 106	jumping rope	1–3 min.	5–10 min.
p. 115	hands behind back	1 x 30 sec. hold	2 x 30–60 sec. hold
p. 113	double wood chop	1 x 30 sec. hold	2 x 30–60 sec. hold
p. 117	palm tree	1 x 30 sec. hold	2 x 30–60 sec. hold
p. 122	inverted figure 4	1 x 30 sec. hold	2 x 30–60 sec. hold
p. 124	quad stretch	1 x 30 sec. hold	2 x 30–60 sec. hold
p. 126	standing hip flexor	1 x 30 sec. hold	2 x 30–60 sec. hold
p. 128	ankle circle	30 sec.	30–60 sec.
p. 130	mad cat	1 x 30 sec. hold	2 x 30–60 sec. hold
p. 123	the butterfly	1 x 30 sec. hold	2 x 30–60 sec. hold

A AGILITY **F** FLEXIBILITY

W WARM-UP **C** CONDITIONING **CR** CORE **B** BALANCE **A** AGILITY **T** TOSS **F** FLEXIBILITY

RUNNING/JOGGING

SKIING: CROSS-COUNTRY

Cross-country skiing is one of the most aerobic events known to the human body. You must have a solid base of fitness before you can engage in this high-intensity sport, therefore it's critical that you train to play. Don't be foolish and think you can compete without preparing your body beforehand.

Pre-season training should start four to six weeks before the season starts. Training should be done three days a week with one day of rest between workouts. Create a program that corrects any muscle imbalances. The in-season focus should be on your sports training; gym-time intensity can be downsized to two days a week if you are skiing a lot.

SKIING: CROSS-COUNTRY

		Untrained/ Off season	Trained/ In season
p. 54	forward lunge with rotator cuff	1 x 5	2 x 10–15
p. 55	arm swing with neck turn	1 x 5	2 x 10–15
p. 56	heel/toe raise	1 x 5	2 x 10–15
p. 59	lunge with horizontal press	1 x 5	2 x 10–15
p. 60	side lunge with upright row	1 x 5	2 x 10–15
p. 65	half-squat with lateral/frontal raise	1 x 5	2 x 10–15
p. 61	bench step-up	1 x 5	2 x 10–15
p. 72	pull-up	1 x 5	2 x 10–15
p. 74	chin-up	1 x 5	2 x 10–15
p. 71	dip	1 x 5	2 x 10–15
p. 83	back extension over ball	1 x 5	2 x 10–15
p. 86	plank	1 x 15 sec. hold	2 x 30–60 sec. hold
p. 81	pointer series	1 x 5	2 x 10–15
p. 78	curl-up	1 x 5	2 x 10–15
p. 91	lunge & twist	1 x 5	2 x 10–15

SKIING: CROSS-COUNTRY

				Untrained/ Off season	Trained/ In season
B		p. 93	bike ride	1 x for 10–30 sec.	2 x for 30–60 sec.
		p. 92	stork stand	1 x 10–30 sec. hold	2 x 30–60 sec. hold
		p. 98	one-leg hop & hold	1 x 10–15	2 x 15–30
		p. 94	heel-toe stand	1 x 30 sec.	1 x 60 sec.
A		p. 103	side-to-side hops	1 x 10–30	2 x 30–60
F		p. 117	palm tree	1 x 30 sec. hold	2 x 30–60 sec. hold
		p. 124	quad stretch	1 x 30 sec. hold	2 x 30–60 sec. hold
		p. 123	the butterfly	1 x 30 sec. hold	2 x 30–60 sec. hold
		p. 125	outer thigh stretch	1 x 30 sec. hold	2 x 30–60 sec. hold
		p. 128	ankle circle	30 sec.	30–60 sec.
		p. 127	rear calf stretch	1 x 30 sec. hold	2 x 30–60 sec. hold

W WARM-UP	**C** CONDITIONING	**CR** CORE	**B** BALANCE	**A** AGILITY	**T** TOSS	**F** FLEXIBILITY

SKIING: DOWNHILL

Downhill skiing is one of the most enjoyable sports around. However, it is also a high-risk sport and you must be fit to play. Being sedentary and then hitting slopes without being trained is dangerous and foolish. When you combine cold air, high altitudes with 50-plus bodies, injuries happen. Downhill skiing requires total strength development of the legs, gluteals, abs and lower back, as well as cardiovascular fitness. Power, strength, endurance, flexibility, reaction time and balance all come into play in this sport.

Pre-season training should start four to six weeks before the season starts. Training should be done three days a week with one day of rest between workouts. Create a program that corrects any muscle imbalances. The in-season focus should be on your sports training; gym-time intensity can be downsized to two days a week if you are skiing a lot.

			Untrained/ Off season	Trained/ In season
W	p. 53	side lunge with frontal/lateral raise	1 x 5	2 x 10–15
	p. 54	forward lunge with rotator cuff	1 x 5	2 x 10–15
	p. 56	heel/toe raise	1 x 5	2 x 10–15
C	p. 59	lunge with horizontal press	1 x 5	2 x 10–15
	p. 60	side lunge with upright row	1 x 5	2 x 10–15
	p. 61	bench step-up	1 x 5	2 x 10–15
	p. 64	squat with dumbbell	1 x 5	2 x 10–15
	p. 65	half-squat with lateral/frontal raise	1 x 5	2 x 10–15
	p. 73	inverted pull-up	1 x 5	2 x 10–15
CR	p. 78	curl-up	1 x 5	2 x 10–15
	p. 81	pointer series	1 x 5	2 x 10–15
	p. 84	pelvic lift	1 x 5	2 x 10–15
	p. 88	twist with band	1 x 5	2 x 10–15
	p. 91	lunge & twist	1 x 5	2 x 10–15
A	p. 101	stair jump	1 x 10–30	2 x 30–60

SKIING: DOWNHILL

			Untrained/ Off season	Trained/ In season
A		p. 103 side-to-side hops	1 x 10–30	2 x 30–60
		p. 104 double-leg hops	1 x 10–30	2 x 30–60
F		p. 118 twister	1 x 30 sec. hold	2 x 30–60 sec. hold
		p. 117 palm tree	1 x 30 sec. hold	2 x 30–60 sec. hold
		p. 124 quad stretch	1 x 30 sec. hold	2 x 30–60 sec. hold
		p. 120 double-leg stretch	1 x 30 sec. hold	2 x 30–60 sec. hold
		p. 123 the butterfly	1 x 30 sec. hold	2 x 30–60 sec. hold
		p. 130 mad cat	1 x 30 sec. hold	2 x 30–60 sec. hold
		p. 127 rear calf stretch	1 x 30 sec. hold	2 x 30–60 sec. hold

W WARM-UP   **C** CONDITIONING   **CR** CORE   **B** BALANCE   **A** AGILITY   **T** TOSS   **F** FLEXIBILITY

SOCCER

Soccer requires muscular endurance and a proper balance of both upper body and core strength. Soccer players must be able to jump, change direction quickly and run. Flexibility, agility, coordination and superior aerobic endurance are central to good performance in your sport. Train to prevent injuries. Your fitness goals will depend upon the position you play. Goal keepers need leg strength, upper body flexibility and jumping power. Strikers require neck strength and strong legs for jumping. Outside fullbacks, wings and midfielders need muscular endurance and great cardiovascular endurance.

Pre-season training should start four to six weeks before the season starts. Training should be done three days a week with one day of rest between workouts. Create a program that corrects any muscle imbalances. The in-season focus should be on your sports training; gym-time intensity can be downsized to two days a week if you are playing a lot. But don't forget to stretch!

			Untrained/ Off season	Trained/ In season
W	p. 52	knee lift	1 x 30 sec.	2 x 60 sec.
	p. 53	side lunge with frontal/lateral raise	1 x 5	2 x 10–15
	p. 54	forward lunge with rotator cuff	1 x 5	2 x 10–15
	p. 56	heel/toe raise	1 x 5	2 x 10–15
C	p. 59	lunge with horizontal press	1 x 5	2 x 10–15
	p. 61	bench step-up	1 x 5	2 x 10–15
	p. 64	squat with dumbbell	1 x 5	2 x 10–15
	p. 65	half-squat with lateral/frontal raise	1 x 5	2 x 10–15
	p. 68	clapping push-up	1 x 5	2 x 10–15
	p. 73	inverted pull-up	1 x 5	2 x 10–15
	p. 75	reverse fly	1 x 5	2 x 10–15
	p. 76	bench press on ball	1 x 5	2 x 10–15
CR	p. 78	curl-up	1 x 5	2 x 10–15
	p. 79	diagonal curl-up	1 x 5	2 x 10–15
	p. 83	back extension over ball	1 x 5	2 x 10–15

SOCCER

SOCCER

			Untrained/ Off season	Trained/ In season
CR	p. 86	plank	1 x 15 sec. hold	2 x 30–60 sec. hold
	p. 88	twist with band	1 x 5	2 x 10–15
	p. 91	lunge & twist	1 x 5	2 x 10–15
B	p. 96	forward jump & hold	1 x 10–15	2 x 15–30
	p. 95	weight shift on soft surface	1 x for 10–30 sec.	2 x for 30–60 sec.
	p. 97	lateral jump & hold	1 x 10–15	2 x 15–30
A	p. 106	jumping rope	1–3 min.	5–10 min.
	p. 103	side-to-side hops	1 x 10–30	2 x 30–60
	p. 105	single-leg hops	1 x 10–30	2 x 30–60
	p. 104	double-leg hops	1 x 10–30	2 x 30–60
T	p. 109	military press & catch	1 x 5	2 x 10–15
	p. 108	bench press & catch	1 x 5	2 x 10–15
F	p. 118	twister	1 x 30 sec. hold	2 x 30–60 sec. hold
	p. 120	double-leg stretch	1 x 30 sec. hold	2 x 30–60 sec. hold
	p. 123	the butterfly	1 x 30 sec. hold	2 x 30–60 sec. hold
	p. 125	outer thigh stretch	1 x 30 sec. hold	2 x 30–60 sec. hold
	p. 128	ankle circle	30 sec.	30–60 sec.
	p. 127	rear calf stretch	1 x 30 sec. hold	2 x 30–60 sec. hold

SOCCER

W WARM-UP **C** CONDITIONING **CR** CORE **B** BALANCE **A** AGILITY **T** TOSS **F** FLEXIBILITY

SWIMMING

Swimming requires explosive power, muscular endurance and cardiovascular endurance—the particulars will vary upon your stroke and your event. Tweaking your form is an on-going battle but well worth it, especially with regard to injury prevention.

   The prevalence of shoulder problems for people over 50 is very high, even among those who don't swim. The repetitive movements of swimming can therefore really mess up a swimmer's goals. Think injury prevention at all times and strive for quality workouts over quantity. Swimmers should focus on arm depressor exercises, elbow extensor exercises, wrist flexor exercises, a solid core, and strong but flexible shoulders. Breaststrokers need to work on adductor muscles. Your gym workout should aim to undo all the forward pull on your chest and shoulders that gives many swimmers a rounded-shoulder appearance.

   Pre-season training should start four to six weeks before the season starts. Training should be done three days a week with one day of rest between workouts. Create a program that corrects any muscle imbalances. The in-season focus should be on your sports training; gym-time intensity can be downsized to two days a week if you are swimming a lot. But don't forget to stretch!

			Untrained/ Off season	Trained/ In season
W	p. 54	forward lunge with rotator cuff	1 x 5	2 x 10–15
	p. 55	arm swing with neck turn	1 x 5	2 x 10–15
	p. 52	knee lift	1 x 30 sec.	2 x 60 sec.
C	p. 60	side lunge with upright row	1 x 5	2 x 10–15
	p. 65	half-squat with lateral/frontal raise	1 x 5	2 x 10–15
	p. 68	wide push-up	1 x 5	2 x 10–15
	p. 70	pilates push-up	1 x 5	2 x 10–15
	p. 71	chair dip	1 x 5	2 x 10–15
	p. 75	reverse fly	1 x 5	2 x 10–15
	p. 72	pull-up	1 x 5	2 x 10–15
	p. 73	inverted pull-up	1 x 5	2 x 10–15
	p. 77	military press on ball	1 x 5	2 x 10–15
CR	p. 78	curl-up	1 x 5	2 x 10–15

SWIMMING

SWIMMING

				Untrained/ Off season	Trained/ In season
CR		*p. 80*	ball roll-out	1 x 5	2 x 10–15
		p. 81	pointer series	1 x 5	2 x 10–15
		p. 74	reverse fly	1 x 5	2 x 10–15
		p. 84	pelvic lift	1 x 5	2 x 10–15
		p. 86	plank	1 x 15 sec. hold	2 x 30–60 sec. hold
A		*p. 99*	speed play	1 x 10–12	1 x 15–20
F		*p. 116*	the zipper	1 x 30 sec. hold	2 x 30–60 sec. hold
		p. 114	choker	1 x 30 sec. hold	2 x 30–60 sec. hold
		p. 115	hands behind back	1 x 30 sec. hold	2 x 30–60 sec. hold
		p. 128	ankle circle	30 sec.	30–60 sec.
		p. 127	rear calf stretch	1 x 30 sec. hold	2 x 30–60 sec. hold

W WARM-UP   **C** CONDITIONING   **CR** CORE   **B** BALANCE   **A** AGILITY   **T** TOSS   **F** FLEXIBILITY

TENNIS

Tennis is an explosive, full-body sport that requires agility and quick bursts of speed and power. It also depends on adequate aerobic stamina to endure long sets. In tennis, the knees can take a great deal of pounding and the shoulders need to reach and stretch in all directions. The load placed on the back is tremendous. Tennis is a one-sided game for most players, thus creating muscle imbalances. So off-the-court training must include stretching what is tight and strengthening what is weak.

Once you establish a baseline of fitness, your program should evolve into a training program that replicates the speed and movements used on the court. Unfortunately, the over-50 body can easily get hurt with ballistic moves if unprepared or untrained.

Additionally, too many recreational tennis players play tennis to get into shape, which is dangerous. The smart person gets in shape to play. Keep in mind that while tennis seems harmless, it's a risky sport and orthopedic injuries can and do happen. Do everything you can to prevent an injury—stay well trained and hydrated.

			Untrained/ Off season	Trained/ In season
W	p. 57	knee to chest	1 x 5	2 x 10–15
	p. 53	side lunge with frontal/lateral raise	1 x 5	2 x 10–15
	p. 54	forward lunge with rotator cuff	1 x 5	2 x 10–15
	p. 56	heel/toe raise	1 x 5	2 x 10–15
C	p. 59	lunge with horizontal press	1 x 5	2 x 10–15
	p. 61	bench side-step	1 x 5	2 x 10–15
	p. 65	half-squat with lateral/frontal raise	1 x 5	2 x 10–15
	p. 66	double-leg thrust with push-up	1 x 5	2 x 10–15
	p. 73	inverted pull-up	1 x 5	2 x 10–15
	p. 75	reverse fly	1 x 5	2 x 10–15
	p. 76	bench press on ball	1 x 5	2 x 10–15
CR	p. 79	diagonal curl-up	1 x 5	2 x 10–15
	p. 80	ball roll-out	1 x 5	2 x 10–15
	p. 83	back extension over ball	1 x 5	2 x 10–15
	p. 85	pelvic lift with leg extension	1 x 5	2 x 10–15

TENNIS

			Untrained/ Off season	Trained/ In season
CR	p. 89	downward chopping	1 x 5	2 x 10–15
	p. 91	lunge & twist	1 x 5	2 x 10–15
B	p. 97	lateral jump & hold	1 x 10–15	2 x 15–30
	p. 98	one-leg hop & hold	1 x 10–15	2 x 15–30
	p. 94	heel-toe stand	30 sec.	60 sec.
A	p. 103	side-to-side hops	1 x 10–30	2 x 30–
	p. 100	lateral shuffle	1 x 10–30	2 x 30–60
	p. 107	superball bounce	1 x 5	2 x 10–15
T	p. 111	throwing motion with band	1 x 5	2 x 10–15
F	p. 116	the zipper	1 x 30 sec. hold	2 x 30–60 sec. hold
	p. 114	choker	1 x 30 sec. hold	2 x 30–60 sec. hold
	p. 117	palm tree	1 x 30 sec. hold	2 x 30–60 sec. hold
	p. 120	double-leg stretch	1 x 30 sec. hold	2 x 30–60 sec. hold
	p. 121	roll into a ball	1 x 30 sec. hold	2 x 30–60 sec. hold
	p. 124	quad stretch	1 x 30 sec. hold	2 x 30–60 sec. hold
	p. 128	ankle circle	30 sec.	30–60 sec.
	p. 129	wrist stretch standing	1 x 30 sec. hold	2 x 30–60 sec. hold
	p. 127	rear calf stretch	1 x 30 sec. hold	2 x 30–60 sec. hold
	p. 119	cross-leg drop	1 x 30 sec. hold	2 x 30–60 sec. hold

W WARM-UP **C** CONDITIONING **CR** CORE **B** BALANCE **A** AGILITY **T** TOSS **F** FLEXIBILITY

part 3:
the
exercises

warm-ups
knee lift

STARTING POSITION: Stand tall with good posture.

starting position

1 March in place, gradually lifting your knees higher as you warm up.

2 As you limber up, swing your arms in opposition as you lift your knees.

side lunge with frontal/lateral raise *target: quads, shoulders*

STARTING POSITION: Stand tall with good posture, keeping your arms in front of your body.

starting position

1 Step your left foot out to the side and raise your arms in front of you to shoulder height.

2 Lower your arms and return your left foot to starting position.

3 Step your right foot out to the side and raise your arms out to the sides until they're shoulder height.

warm-ups

forward lunge with rotator cuff   *target: quads, shoulders*

This can be done with or without dumbbells.

STARTING POSITION: Stand tall with good posture. Bend your arms 90 degrees with your palms facing in. Keep your elbows pinned to your ribs throughout the exercise.

starting position

1

1 Step your right foot forward into a comfortable lunge and move your palms outward; make sure your knee stays behind your toes.

2

2 Step back into starting position.

3 Step forward into a lunge with your left foot and move your palms outward.

3

warm-ups
arm swing with neck turn
target: shoulders, neck

55

CAUTION: *Perform this move slowly and with control. If you have neck issues, get clearance from your doctor before doing this.*

STARTING POSITION: Stand tall with your arms along your sides.

starting position

1 Gently swing your left arm forward as you swing your right arm backward, moving your arms as high as they can easily go. Gently look to the right.

2 Return to starting position.

3 Gently swing your right arm forward and look to the left while your right arm moves backward.

STARTING POSITION: Stand tall with your arms by your sides.

starting position

1

2

3

1 Raise your heels off the floor and hold for 1–3 seconds.

2 Lower yourself to starting position.

3 Roll back onto your heels until your toes are off the ground; hold for 1–3 seconds.

Lower and repeat the sequence.

MODIFICATION

If you have balance issues, you can raise your arms out to your sides or you can hold on to something such as a chair or the wall.

CAUTION: *If you don't have good balance, please perform this move while lying on your back.*

STARTING POSITION: Stand tall.

starting position

1 Lift your right leg up as high as is comfortable; reach under your leg/knee and hug it to your chest for 3–5 seconds.

2 Lower slowly to the starting position and switch sides.

Continue performing this move.

lower body
lunge with vertical press

target: quads, shoulders

STARTING POSITION: Stand tall with your feet shoulder-width apart and hold a dumbbell in each hand. Bend your elbows 90 degrees and bring the dumbbells in line with your shoulders; your palms should face forward.

starting position

1 With your left leg, step forward into a lunge and bend your right knee to the floor or as low as is comfortable; press both dumbbells up toward the ceiling. Make sure your front knee stays behind your toes.

2 Return to starting position.

3 Continue with the left before switching sides.

VARIATION
You can also perform this as a backward lunge. Step one foot backward and lower that knee to the floor so that your front leg is in a good lunge.

lunge with horizontal press

target: quads, shoulders

STARTING POSITION: Stand tall with your feet shoulder-width apart and hold a dumbbell in each hand. Bend your elbows 90 degrees and bring the dumbbells in line with your shoulders; your palms should face down.

starting position

1 With your left leg, step forward into a lunge and lower your right knee to the floor as low as is comfortable; press both dumbbells forward. Make sure your front knee stays behind your toes.

2 Return to starting position.

3 Continue with the left before switching sides.

VARIATION

You can also perform this as a backward lunge. Step one foot backward and lower that knee to the floor so that your front leg is in a good lunge.

TIPS

• Keep your core stable and maintain control of your posture.

lower body

side lunge with upright row

target: quads, shoulders

STARTING POSITION: Stand tall with good posture. Holding a dumbbell in each hand, let your arms hang in front of you with your palms in front of your thighs.

starting position

1 Step your left foot out to the side and bend your knee, keeping it behind your toes; bring the dumbbells up in front of your torso as if you were using it as a washboard. Your elbows should flare out at the top of the movement.

2 Lower your arms as you return to starting position.

3 Step your right foot out to the side and perform the upright row.

CAUTION: If you experience any knee joint discomfort or swelling, discontinue this exercise and perform half squats (page 65), with or without weights, instead.

STARTING POSITION: Stand tall facing a sturdy bench, step or staircase.

starting position

1 Step your right foot onto the step.

2 Return to starting position.

3 Step your left foot onto the step.

Continue alternating legs.

1

2

3

MODIFICATION
As your strength increases, you can increase the height of the step, hold a dumbbell in both hands or wear a weighted vest.

TIPS
• Make sure your kneecap does not angle to the left or right when stepping.
• Keep your knee behind your big toe when stepping.

STARTING POSITION: Stand with the left side of your body next to a sturdy bench, step or staircase.

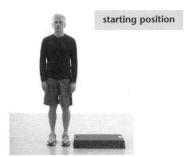

starting position

1 Step your left foot onto the platform, leaving enough room for your right foot.

2 Step your right foot next to your left.

3 Step down with your right foot.

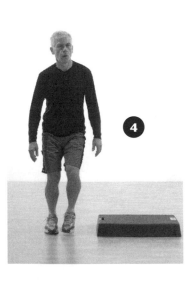

4 Step down with your left foot.

Repeat by standing with your right side to the step.

double-leg lift

target: back, buttocks

Make sure you have plenty of space to perform this move.

STARTING POSITION: Lie face down with your belly button centered over the middle of the ball. Place your hands on the floor for support. Maintain neutral spine position throughout the movement by tightening your abs.

starting position

1 Lift both legs up to the height of your rear end and hold for 3–5 seconds.

2 Slowly lower to starting position and reposition your body, checking for neutral spine position before repeating.

VARIATION
This can also be done by lifting one leg at a time. You can also try lifting your right arm and left leg, and then switch sides.

lower body
squat with dumbbell

Squats foster greater leg strength and provide stabilization to compromised knee joints.

STARTING POSITION: Stand tall with your feet shoulder-width apart. Hold a dumbbell between your legs.

starting position

1 Keeping your back in neutral spine position, bend your knees to lower your rear end into a half-squat. Make sure your knees stay behind your toes.

2 Return to starting position.

MODIFICATION
For more support, you can sit into a chair and then get up.

STARTING POSITION: Stand tall with your feet shoulder-width apart. With your ams along your sides, hold a dumbbell in each hand.

starting position

1 Keeping your back in neutral spine position, bend your knees to lower your rear end into a half-squat and lift the weights out to your sides until they're shoulder height.

2 Return to starting position.

3 Lower into a half-squat and raise the weights forward to shoulder height.

Continue doing squats, alternating between lateral and frontal raises.

MODIFICATION
For more support, you can sit into a chair and then get up.

TIPS
- Do not lose neutral spine posture.
- Do not use momentum to swing the weights upward.
- Do not raise your arms above your shoulders.

lower body
double-leg thrust with push-up
target: legs, shoulders, arms

CAUTION: This exercise is only for advanced athletes with no joint issues.

STARTING POSITION: Stand with your feet shoulder-width apart.

starting position

1

2

3

4

5

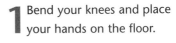
1 Bend your knees and place your hands on the floor.

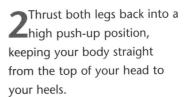
2 Thrust both legs back into a high push-up position, keeping your body straight from the top of your head to your heels.

3 Bend your elbows to perform a standard push-up.

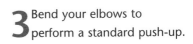
4 Keeping your hands on the floor, jump your feet to your hands.

5 Return to starting position.

MODIFICATION
If you are unable to do a push-up, stop at step 2 and return to starting position.

Push-ups improve the muscular strength and endurance of the chest and triceps. They can also be excellent core stabilizers when the torso is held firmly. If you have wrist issues, you may want to invest in commercially available push-up handles.

starting position

STARTING POSITION: Lie face down on the floor with your hands besides your shoulders and your legs extended behind you. Press your toes into the floor.

1 Press your hands into the floor to lift your chest and torso. Keep your body rigid, forming a straight line from your head to your heels.

2 Lower your chest until it's an inch or two from the floor; do not allow your chest to rest on the floor.

3 Press your chest away from the floor until your arms are straight.

MODIFICATION
Beginners can perform this from their knees or by placing their hands on a wall, table or chair.

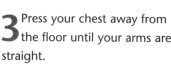

TIPS
• Keep your core engaged and maintain good posture—do not sag or pike in the middle.

SINGLE-ARM VARIATION: Strong, advanced individuals who do not have shoulder issues, high blood pressure or heart issues can perform this, too: while in push-up position, lift one arm slightly off the floor and hold for 1–3 seconds. Alternate arms.

Single-arm variation

ADVANCED VARIATION: Pause in down position for 1–2 seconds; do not hold your breath.

Advanced variation

DIAMOND VARIATION: To focus on the triceps and the part of the chest closest to the breast bone, place your hands on the floor and create a diamond/triangle shape with your hands by touching the index finger and thumb of each hand together.

Diamond variation

WIDE VARIATION: To target the outer portion of your chest, place your hands as wide as possible on the floor.

Wide variation

CLAPPING VARIATION: To develop explosive power in the chest and shoulder region, push your chest off the ground as hard as you can and clap your hands together before returning them to the floor.

Clapping variation

UNSTEADY VARIATION: To improve core stability and upper body strength and dynamic balance of your entire body, place your hands on two unstable pads and perform push-ups. Once you lose perfect form, STOP! The purpose of this activity is total integration of the arms, legs and torso.

Unsteady variation

Props can be used to change the intensity and target muscles of your push-ups.

DECLINE CHAIR VARIATION: This push-up focuses on the upper region of the chest and shoulder complex. Keeping your hands on the floor in normal push-up position, place your feet on a stable chair.

INCLINE CHAIR VARIATION: This push-up focuses on the lower region of the chest and shoulder complex. Keeping your feet on the floor, place both hands on a chair.

BLOCK VARIATION: Place your hands on blocks (these can be purchased at sporting goods stores) while keeping your feet on the floor.

STANDING-BEHIND-CHAIR VARIATION: If you're not ready for any of the previous options, stand behind a chair, place your hands on its back and perform push-ups until your strength increases.

TIPS

• Keep your core engaged and maintain good posture—do not sag or pike in the middle.

This push-up focuses on stabilization of the core and shoulder complex.

STARTING POSITION: Begin in standard push-up position, with your hands and balls of your feet on the floor and your body forming a straight line from head to heels.

starting position

1 Rotate your body to the left, lifting your right arm to the ceiling. Make sure to stack your hips.

2 Return to regular push-up position.

3 Lower your chest until it's an inch or two from the floor.

4 Press up and rotate your body to the right, lifting your left hand to the ceiling. Make sure to stack your hips.

5 Return to regular push-up position.

TIPS

• Keep your core engaged and maintain good posture—do not sag or pike in the middle.

CAUTION: If you feel discomfort in your elbows or shoulders, stop immmediately.

STARTING POSITION: Place your hands on the parallel dip bars. Lift your body until your arms are straight.

starting position

1 Keeping your elbows close to your body, lower your body until your elbows bend 90 degrees.

2 Lift your body up to starting position

CHAIR VARIATION

Place the heels of your hands on the front of a sturdy chair, letting your fingers hang off the edge; your rear end should rest against the edge and your legs should be far enough away from the chair to form a 90-degree angle. To do the dip, let your rear end drop off the edge and lower it towards the floor.

TIPS

- Do not allow your elbows to bend beyond 90 degrees.
- If you experience any discomfort in your elbows, stop.
- Be careful that the chair does not tip over.

upper body

pull-up

target: shoulders, biceps, forearms, upper back

In addition to strengthening the upper body, pull-ups also help build muscular endurance. Holding the core and torso in correct form challenges the midsection.

STARTING POSITION: Grab the pull-up bar with your hands shoulder-width apart and palms facing forward.

starting position

1

2

1 Keeping your body straight and looking straight ahead, contract your arm muscles and pull your body upward until your chin reaches bar height.

2 Slowly lower your body until your arms are straight.

NARROW-GRIP VARIATION

Take a narrow grip, with your hands about 4 inches apart.

WIDE-GRIP VARIATION

This version targets the lats more. Grab the bar with your hands spread as wide as is comfortable.

PROGRESSION

Once you are able to perform 10 reps, wear ankle weights or a weighted vest.

TIPS

• Avoid using momentum to assist you.

STARTING POSITION: Lie on the floor and extend your arms toward the ceiling; adjust the pull-up bar so that it's just a few inches above your arms. Grab the bar with your hands shoulder-width apart.

starting position

1 Keeping your body rigid, pull your body up toward bar; pause at the top.

2 Slowly lower your body.

MODIFICATION
To improve grip strength, loop two small towels over the bar. Grab the towels to perform the motion.

This exercise strengthens the upper body and improves grip strength.

STARTING POSITION: Grab the pull-up bar with your hands shoulder-width apart and your palms facing your body.

starting position

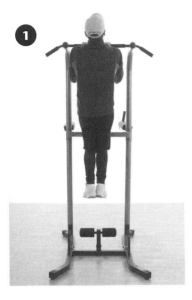

1 Keeping your body straight and looking straight ahead, contract your arm muscles and lift your body upward until your chin reaches bar height.

2 Slowly lower your body until your arms are straight.

NARROW-GRIP VARIATION

Bring your hands as close together as is comfortable.

OVER-UNDER VARIATION

Grab the bar with one palm facing forward and the other facing your body. Perform repetitions using this grip, rest, then switch the grip.

PROGRESSION

Once you are able to perform 10 reps, wear ankle weights.

TIPS

• Avoid using momentum to assist you.

This exercise improves upper back posture; performing it on the ball enhances core stability. It is especially good for swimmers. Be sure to find a safe, spacious place to perform this move.

STARTING POSITION: Holding a dumbbell in each hand, lie on your stomach with your belly button centered on or close to the middle of the ball. Extend your legs behind you until your feet/toes are touching the ground. Maintain proper posture throughout the exercise by pulling your shoulder blades together and keeping your spine neutral.

starting position

1 Slowly lift your arms out to your sides to form a "T."

2 Slowly return to starting position.

①

②

VARIATION
For an extra challenge, use your arms to also form the letters "I" and "Y."

upper body
bench press on ball

target: chest, shoulders, core

STARTING POSITION: Holding a dumbbell in each hand, place your midback on the ball with your feet on the floor; your knees should be about hip-width apart. Hold the dumbbells just above either shoulder, palms facing the ceiling. Tighten your abs to maintain a straight back throughout the exercise.

starting position

1 Press the weights straight up to the ceiling.

2 Lower the dumbbells to your chest.

TIPS
• Make sure your back does not arch or sag.

military press on ball

target: core, shoulders

STARTING POSITION: Sit on the ball in a balanced position with your feet flat on the floor. Bend your elbows 90 degrees and bring the dumbbells in line with your shoulders; your palms should face forward.

starting position

1 Press the weights straight up to the ceiling.

2 While keeping your core muscles contracted, lower the weights to starting position.

TIPS

• Do not arch or let your back sag.

core
curl-up

STARTING POSITION: Lie on the floor with your knees bent and your hands gently supporting your head.

starting position

1 Using your pelvic muscles, exhale and gently press your lower back into the floor, contracting your abdominal muscles and curling/lifting your upper back and shoulders off the floor. Hold at the top of the lift for 1–2 seconds.

2 Inhale and slowly return to starting position.

TIPS
- Don't force the motion or use your arms to assist the movement.
- Don't hold your breath.

STARTING POSITION: Lie on the floor with your knees bent and your hands gently supporting your head.

starting position

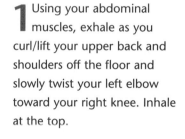

1 Using your abdominal muscles, exhale as you curl/lift your upper back and shoulders off the floor and slowly twist your left elbow toward your right knee. Inhale at the top.

2 Exhale and slowly return to starting position.

3 Curl your upper back and shoulders off the floor and slowly twist your right elbow to your left knee.

TIPS
- Gently lower your upper body.
- Keep a slow and steady pace.

This motion teaches you better control of your core when doing compound motions.

STARTING POSITION: Lie on your back in proper neutral spine posture and place your heels on the ball. Your arms can be extended along your sides for support.

1 Maintaining neutral spine, extend your legs to roll the ball outward, stopping before you lose good posture; hold.

2 Slowly roll the ball back to starting position.

MODIFICATION
You can do this using one leg at a time until you are able to use both legs. If this is still too challenging, you can keep your back and bottom on the floor as you perform the roll-out.

Be sure to find a safe, spacious place to perform this move.

STARTING POSITION: Lie face down with your belly button centered over the middle of the ball. Place your hands and toes lightly on the floor for support.

1 Slowly lift your right arm to shoulder height and hold for 1–3 seconds.

2 Slowly lower to starting position.

3 Slowly lift your left arm to shoulder height and hold for 1–3 seconds.

4 Slowly lower to starting position.

5 Lift both arms and hold for 1–3 seconds.

This advanced exercise fosters proper upper back posture and reverses the rounded/hunched back that comes with overly inflexible chest muscles. It also requires core strength and balance.

STARTING POSITION: Lie face down with your belly button centered over the middle of the ball; raise your legs until they're parallel to the floor. Your fingertips provide only light assistance for balance.

starting position

1 Lift your left arm parallel to the ground and touch your left toes to the ground; hold.

2 Now switch so that your other arm comes up and your other foot goes down.

Continue switching, maintaining proper form.

core
back extension over ball

target: lower back

83

STARTING POSITION: Lie face down on the ball with your belly button slightly forward of center and your feet gently touching the floor for support. Place your hands lightly behind your head.

starting position

1 Raise your torso off the ball.

2 Return to starting posItion.

TIPS

• Do not perform this move quickly.
• Do not arch your back—only come up to a straight position.

STARTING POSITION: Lie on your back with your knees bent and arms alongside your body; gently press your lower back into the floor.

starting position

1 Press your feet into the ground to slowly lift your rear end and lower back off the floor; you will ultimately form a nice line from your shoulders to your hips.

2 Lower your body until it's 1 inch from the ground.

3 Repeat.

BALL VARIATION
To further challenge the muscles of the lower back and buttocks, perform the pelvic lift by placing your feet on the ball. Be sure to maintain proper shoulder and hip alignment.

This advanced exercise will improve core stabilization of the whole mid-section area.

STARTING POSITION: Lie on your back with your knees bent and arms alongside your body.

starting position

1 Press your feet into the ground to slowly lift your rear end and lower back off the floor; you will ultimately form a nice line from your shoulders to your hips.

2 Slowly straighten your left leg from the knee joint until it's diagonal to the ground; hold this position for 5–10 seconds.

3 Lower your body to the ground.

4 Place your left foot on the ground.

Repeat the sequence using the other leg.

TIPS

- Do not perform this movement quickly.
- If you feel a cramp coming on, stop and stretch your hamstrings.

This is an advanced exercise that must be done properly to engage all the muscles of the core.

CAUTION: Do not perform this move if you have high blood pressure or a hernia.

POSITION: Assume a modified push-up position by placing your forearms shoulder-width apart on the floor and extending your legs behind you to balance on the balls of your feet. Maintain this position for the recommended time, breathing comfortably.

VARIATION
For an extra challenge, try lifting one leg and then the other.

TIPS
• Do not hold your breath.
• Contract your midsection to prevent from sagging.

This advanced exercise requires total mind-body engagement of the core.

CAUTION: Do not perform this if you have shoulder joint issues or cardiovascular concerns.

POSITION: Lying on the left side of your body, position your elbow under your shoulder to prop yourself up.

starting position

1 Contract your midsection and press your forearm into the floor to lift your hips off the floor. Assume a straight line from your ankles to your shoulders. Maintain this position for for the recommended time. Come down to rest, then switch sides.

This can be done while seated or standing.

CAUTION: If you have back issues, speak to a health provider about doing this exercise.

STARTING POSITION: Secure an elastic band to a sturdy, stable object so that it is at chest level. Stand tall with your left side to the band. Hold the band with both hands and extend your arms straight out in front of you at chest level.

starting position

1 Slowly twist to the right.

2 Return to starting position and repeat.

Reposition yourself to perform this move in the other direction.

1

2

MODIFICATION
This move can also be performed by holding dumbbells.

CAUTION: *If you have back issues, speak to a health provider about doing this exercise.*

STARTING POSITION: Secure an elastic band high on a tall, sturdy object. Stand in a stable athletic stance with your left side to the band. Grasp the band with both hands.

starting position

1 With control, move the band down and across your body at a 45-degree angle, as if chopping a log or swinging a golf club.

2 Slowly return to starting position and repeat.

Reposition yourself to perform this move in the other direction.

core
upward chopping

CAUTION: If you have back issues, speak to a health provider about doing this exercise.

STARTING POSITION: Secure an elastic band low on a sturdy object. Stand in a stable athletic stance with your right side to the band. Grasp the band with both hands.

starting position

1 With control, move the band up and across at a 45-degree angle, as if following through in a golf swing.

2 Slowly return to starting position and repeat.

Reposition yourself to perform this move in the other direction.

CAUTION: If you have back issues, do not do this exercise.

STARTING POSITION: Stand tall with good posture, holding a weight or medicine ball straight out in front of you.

starting position

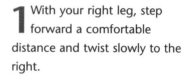

1 With your right leg, step forward a comfortable distance and twist slowly to the right.

2 Return to starting position.

3 Step forward with your left leg while slowly twisting to the right.

Continue alternating legs.

balance

stork stand

target: legs

CAUTION: *Do not do this if you have a history of falling.*

STARTING POSITION: Stand tall with your feet shoulder-width apart and shoulders back.

1 Shift your weight to your right leg and lift your left foot to your right knee. Maintain this posture without movement for the recommended time.

2 Repeat on the opposite leg.

MODIFICATION
To increase the challenge, close your eyes or turn your head slowly to the left and right while maintaining balance.

TIPS
• Concentrate on feeling the ground with your complete foot.
• Keep your eyes open and look straight ahead.

balance
bike ride

CAUTION: *Do not do this if you have a history of falling.*

STARTING POSITION: Stand tall with your feet shoulder-width apart and shoulders back. Hold your arms in front of you as if grasping handlebars.

starting position

1–3 Shift your weight to your right leg and lift your left leg. Pretend that you are riding a bike with only one pedal. Continue for the recommended time.

Rest then repeat with your other leg.

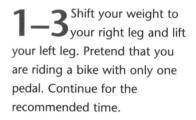

balance
heel-toe stand

CAUTION: Do not do this if you have a history of falling.

POSITION: Stand tall with your right heel in front of your left toes. Maintain this posture for the recommended time, then switch feet position and hold.

MODIFICATION
Once this becomes easy, try closing your eyes while maintaining this position. Once this is easy, turn your head slowly while your eyes are closed.

CAUTION: Do not do this if you have a history of falling.

STARTING POSITION: Stand tall on a soft foam pad with your feet shoulder-width apart and shoulders back. Maintain your balance for a few seconds.

starting position

1 Once this becomes easy, shift your body weight to one foot; hold for 5 seconds.

Continue shifting your weight.

1

balance
forward jump & hold

This exercise will enhance dynamic balance and power.

STARTING POSITION: Stand with your feet about shoulder-width apart in a solid athletic stance.

starting position

1–2 Jump forward, landing on both feet; absorb the shock and maintain balance by keeping your knees soft. Hold for a moment.

3 Jump backwards.

VARIATION
To increase the challenge, you can either try this by jumping from a foam pad or jumping onto a foam pad.

CAUTION: Avoid landing on a soft surface if you have weak ankles.

This movement is designed for athletes who play sports that require a lot of lateral movement, such as tennis.

STARTING POSITION: Stand with your feet about shoulder-width apart in a solid athletic stance.

starting position

1

1 Jump sideways to the left, landing on your left foot and maintaining your balance. Hold for a moment.

2 Jump to the right, landing on your right foot and maintaining your balance. Hold for a moment.

Continue jumping left and right, holding for a moment before performing the next jump.

2

TIPS

• As your ability improves, increase the speed and height of your rebound.

balance
one-leg hop & hold

This exercise will enhance dynamic balance and power. You'll need enough space to move forward.

STARTING POSITION: Stand on your right foot.

starting position

1 Hop forward, landing on your left foot; absorb the shock and maintain balance by keeping your knee soft. Hold for a moment.

Continue hopping forward, this time landing on your right foot. Repeat, alternating feet.

VARIATION

If space is an issue, hop back to your starting position and then hop forward with your other foot.

To make this more challenging, you can use a foam pad to jump to and from.

speed play: hard/easy

The name of this exercise is misleading because it does not actually feel like "play." This very advanced activity challenges the aerobic and anaerobic systems of the body and should not be performed until you have an excellent baseline of fitness and health. This exercise also helps improve performance times. You'll need to go to a local track to do this.

STARTING POSITION: Select a starting line at the point where the track straightens out. Have a stopwatch available to measure times if desired.

1 Sprint as fast as you can down the straightaways.

2 As you enter the curve, slow down the pace dramatically by either jogging or walking the curve.

3 When you are ready, sprint the straightaway as fast as you want.

4 Recover around the curve.

TIPS

• This workout should only be done once or twice a week, well separated by recovery time to avoid injury. This same concept can be applied to biking or swimming (i.e., sprint a set distance and then slow down).

This exercise helps your footwork become more fluid.

STARTING POSITION: Place two targets a good distance from each other. Start at one end, keeping your feet wide and center of gravity low.

starting position

1

1 Keeping your weight low, shuffle smoothly to the other target.

2 Touch the target before shuffling back to the other side.

Continue shuffling for the recommended amount of time.

2

speed, agility & power

stair jump

This activity fosters leg strength and explosive power. You'll need to find a set of stairs, preferably stadium bleachers.

CAUTION: Avoid this activity if you have any orthopedic issues.

STARTING POSITION: Facing the first step, stand with both feet together.

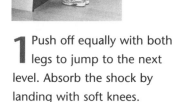
starting position

1 Push off equally with both legs to jump to the next level. Absorb the shock by landing with soft knees.

2 Immediately explode upward and forward again.

Repeat quickly to develop power and agility.

MODIFICATION
As your strength improves, you can try wearing a weighted vest.

This activity improves lateral jumping power. The series of targets can be created by drawing circles on the ground with chalk or placing down pieces of tape.

CAUTION: Avoid this activity if you have any orthopedic issues.

STARTING POSITION: Stand inside one circle or on a target.

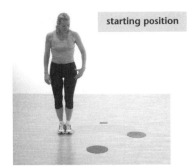

starting position

1 Jump to the next circle/target and hold. After you've jumped the series of circles/targets, jump in the other direction.

Repeat quickly to develop power and agility.

VARIATION
This can also be performed on one leg.

You can also have a partner call out different targets to land on in an unpredictable manner.

MODIFICATION
As your strength improves, you can try wearing a weighted vest.

speed, agility & power
side-to-side hops
103

starting position

CAUTION: *If you have knee or balance issues, do not perform this exercise.*

STARTING POSITION: With your feet on either side of a marker, stand tall with a solid athletic stance.

1 Raise your left heel to your rear end and hop to the right.

2 Return to starting position for a second to regain balance.

3 Quickly raise your right heel to your rear end and hop to the left.

Repeat as quickly as possible for the recommended time or until fatigued.

VARIATION
If you're more advanced, do not stand on both legs—just quickly shift from left to right legs. For the super-advanced, place a 2x4 on the floor and hop left and right over it.

speed, agility & power
double-leg hops
104

CAUTION: *If you have weak ankles, knees or poor balance, start this exercise in the pool.*

STARTING POSITION: Stand in an athletic stance.

starting position

1 Jump as far forward as is comfortable, landing on both feet while maintaining your balance.

2 Jump backwards to the starting point, landing on both legs.

Repeat quickly to develop power and agility.

MODIFICATION
As you advance, try to jump for height instead of distance.

TIPS
• Make sure you push evenly off of both legs.

speed, agility & power
single-leg hops
105

CAUTION: *If you have weak ankles, knees or poor balance, start this exercise in the pool.*

STARTING POSITION: Stand on your left leg.

starting position

1 Jump as far forward as is comfortable, landing on your left foot while maintaining your balance.

2 Jump backwards to the starting point, landing on your left foot.

Switch sides. Repeat quickly to develop power and agility.

MODIFICATION
As you advance, try to jump for height instead of distance.

speed, agility & power
jumping rope

CAUTION: Avoid if you have heart or joint concerns.

STARTING POSITION: Hold a jump rope handle in each hand and stand in front of the rope.

starting position

Option 1: Jump with both feet simultaneously over the rope.

Option 2: Skip over the rope by alternating legs.

Repeat quickly to develop power and agility.

This exercise is great for honing your reflexes.

STARTING POSITION: Hold a very bouncy ball and stand in an athletic ready position (think baseball/softball infielder).

starting position

1

2

1 Toss/throw the ball against a wall.

2 React as quickly as possible to retrieve it.

MODIFICATION
As you advance, stand farther away from the wall or obtain a more reactive ball.

bench press & catch

This is a very advanced move.

CAUTION: Do not perform this if you have poor reaction time, coordination, vision or joint concerns.

STARTING POSITION: Lie on your back with your knees bent and feet flat on the floor. Hold the light medicine ball with both hands.

starting position

1 Press the medicine ball up and into the air as forcefully as you can.

2 Catch the ball, absorbing the shock with your arms as the ball comes down. Immediately explode the ball upward as soon as you have control of the ball.

Repeat for the recommended time or until fatigue occurs.

VARIATION
Use a heavier ball as you improve.

This is a very advanced move.

CAUTION: Do not perform this if you have poor reaction time, coordination or vision.

STARTING POSITION: Standing in an athletic stance with your feet together and knees slightly bent, hold the ball in front of your chest.

starting position

1 Press the medicine ball up as forcefully as you can.

2 Catch the ball, absorbing the shock with your arms as the ball comes down. Immediately explode the ball upward as soon as you have control of the ball, engaging the power of your legs and arms.

Repeat for the recommended time or until fatigue occurs.

power: upper body

under-arm toss

You can also perform this against a wall.

STARTING POSITION: Stand with a solid athletic stance.

1 Using an underhand throw, toss the ball into the air.

2 Catch the ball.

VARIATION

This can also be performed with a two-handed throw.

MODIFICATION

As you progress, toss the ball higher and more quickly.

STARTING POSITION: Attach a band to a stable, sturdy object and grasp the band in your dominant hand. Stand as if you were going to throw a ball overhand.

starting position

1

1–2 Using the band, move as if you are throwing a ball, trying to incorporate proper throwing mechanics.

Repeat on this side then switch to the non-dominant hand.

2

power: upper body
medicine ball throw

This can also be done against a wall.

STARTING POSITION: Stand with a solid athletic stance and hold the medicine ball as if you were going to perform a basketball chest press.

starting position

1–2 Pressing the ball from your chest, throw the ball forward at your partner, who should attempt to catch it and immediately throw it back to you.

Continue for the recommended time.

VARIATION
This can also be performed with an underhand throw.

double wood chop

target: deltoids

STARTING POSITION: Stand with proper posture. Position your hands in front of your body and interlace your fingers.

starting position

1

2

1 Inhale deeply through your nose and slowly raise both arms in front of you to a comfortable height. Hold 1–2 seconds.

2 Slowly lower your arms to starting position.

Repeat.

You can also try this stretch standing with proper posture.

STARTING POSITION: Sit with proper posture in a stable chair.

starting position

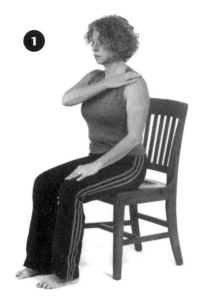

1 Place your right hand on your left shoulder.

2 Place your left hand on your right elbow and gently press your right elbow toward your throat. Hold.

Switch sides and repeat.

VARIATION

In Step 2, press your right elbow into your left hand. Hold for a comfortable moment, remembering to breathe. Then release to reach the right hand a little farther back.

hands behind back

target: shoulders, chest

You can also use a bar instead of a strap.

STARTING POSITION: Stand with proper posture.

starting position

1 Hold the ends of a strap in each hand behind your bottom.

2 Attempt to straighten your arms behind you. Focus on squeezing your shoulder blades together. Hold this position.

ADVANCED

Instead of using a strap, interlock your hands behind your back.

You can also try this stretch standing with proper posture.

STARTING POSITION: Stand with proper posture. Hold a strap in your right hand and raise your arm above your head.

1 Bring your right hand down behind your head and grab the dangling end of the strap with your lower hand.

2 Raise your right hand up as high as possible to lift the lower hand, staying in your pain-free zone. Hold the position.

3 Pull down with the lower hand to bring down the higher hand. Hold the position.

Switch sides and repeat.

ADVANCED

As you become more flexible, eliminate the use of the strap and try to grab your fingertips.

stretches
palm tree

target: torso

You can also try this stretch standing with proper posture.

CAUTION: *If you have poor balance or low back problems, avoid this move.*

STARTING POSITION: Sit with proper posture in a stable chair. Raise your hands overhead with your arms as straight as feels comfortable. Inhale deeply through your nose.

starting position

1 While exhaling through your lips, slowly lean to your left. Hold the position, feeling the stretch along the right side of your body.

2 Now inhale fully and deeply through your nose and lean to your right. Hold this position.

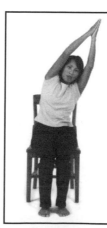

ADVANCED
Try pressing your hands together as you do the side bends.

stretches
twister

You can also try this stretch standing with proper posture.

CAUTION: *Be careful if you have low back problems.*

STARTING POSITION: Sit with proper posture in a stable chair. Cross your arms in front of your chest and inhale slowly and deeply through your nose.

starting position

1 While exhaling through your lips, slowly twist to your left. Hold the position and feel the stretch in your torso.

2 Inhale and return to the starting position before exhaling and twisting to your right. Hold the position and feel the stretch in your torso.

cross-leg drop

target: torso, piriformis

CAUTION: *Be careful if you have low back problems.*

STARTING POSITION: Lie on a mat with your knees bent and your feet flat on the floor.

starting position

1 While focusing on your breathing, place your right knee on top of your left knee.

2 Slowly allow your right knee to gently fall toward the left side. Stop when you feel tightness. Hold this position. The stretch should be felt near the rear pocket area of the right leg. Focus on the stretch, not on how close you can bring the knees to the floor.

Switch sides and repeat.

STARTING POSITION: Sit on a mat, with both legs straight out in front of you and your toes pointing up.

starting position

1

1 Loop a strap around your feet and hold an end of the strap in each hand.

2 Gently pull yourself forward, keeping your back straight while you reach as far forward as is comfortable. Hold, feeling the stretch in your low back and the backs of your legs. Focus on keeping the legs straight.

2

MODIFICATIONS

If you don't have a strap, you can gently press your thighs to the floor, your palms down on your thighs.

If you have a partner, have him/her gently push you forward.

ADVANCED

Interlace your fingers and reach forward, keeping your arms parallel to the floor.

CAUTION: *Do not do this stretch if you have knee problems.*

STARTING POSITION: Place your hands and knees on the floor. Inhale through your nose.

starting position

1 While exhaling deeply through your mouth, slowly allow your bottom to drop toward your heels. If you feel discomfort, you may place a pillow between your heels and bottom.

2 Place your forehead on the floor or a pillow and position your arms alongside your body. Hold this position, enjoying the sensation of the stretch up and down your back.

VARIATION

If you can find a friend to rub up and down your back while doing this stretch, it will enhance the stretch.

ADVANCED

Stretch your arms out straight in front of you.

STARTING POSITION: Lie on a mat with your knees bent and your feet flat on the floor.

starting position

1 Place your left ankle on top of your right knee. Inhale deeply through your nose.

2 Wrap both hands around your right leg and bring your knee and ankle to your chest while exhaling.

3 Now straighten your right leg toward the ceiling as much as is comfortable. Focus on inhaling and exhaling fully and hold this stretch.

Switch sides and repeat.

the butterfly

STARTING POSITION: Sit on a mat with your knees bent and your feet flat on the floor. Place the soles of your feet together and gently allow your knees to drop to the floor.

starting position

1 Loop a strap around your feet and gently pull yourself forward, not down. Hold this stretch.

1

ADVANCED

Place your hands on your ankles and pull yourself forward.

CAUTION: *Avoid this exercise if you have poor balance. STOP if you notice undue compression in your knee or experience any low back discomfort. If you feel a cramp coming on, do a hamstrings stretch.*

STARTING POSITION: Stand with proper posture facing a chair.

starting position

1 Loop a strap around your right ankle and bring your right heel toward your bottom. Keep both knees as close together as possible.

2 Gently pull your heel closer to your bottom, using the back of a chair for balance if necessary. Hold this stretch.

Switch sides and repeat.

INTERMEDIATE

Try this without the strap by grabbing your foot with your hand.

ADVANCED

Try this without the chair, raising your free arm toward the ceiling.

CAUTION: *If you've been advised by your doctor or therapist not to cross your legs, do not do this exercise.*

STARTING POSITION: Stand with proper posture next to a chair on your left side.

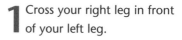

starting position

1 Cross your right leg in front of your left leg.

2 Raise your right arm up overhead and lean to the left, gently pressing your right hip outward to the right. Use the chair for balance. Hold this stretch.

Switch sides and repeat.

VARIATION

If your shoulders are tight, just place your hand on your hips.

ADVANCED

If balance is not an issue, try this without the chair.

stretches
standing hip flexor

target: hip flexors

STARTING POSITION: Stand behind a chair and place your hands on the back of the chair.

starting position

1 Slide your right leg back a comfortable distance. Keeping your rear heel down, gently tuck your tailbone under and press your hips forward. Hold this stretch, focusing on feeling the stretch in the upper leg/hip region rather than in the calf area.

Switch sides and repeat.

tuck your tailbone under

STARTING POSITION: Stand behind a chair, placing both hands on the back of the chair.

starting position

1 Keeping the heel down, slide your right leg as far back as you can.

2 Bend your left knee until the desired stretch is felt in the calf area. Hold this stretch.

Switch sides and repeat.

STARTING POSITION: Sit at the edge of a stable chair.

starting position

1 Cross your right ankle on top of your left knee and gently grasp your right foot with your left hand.

2 Slowly use your hand to gently move your foot in comfortable circles as well as forward and backward.

Switch sides and repeat.

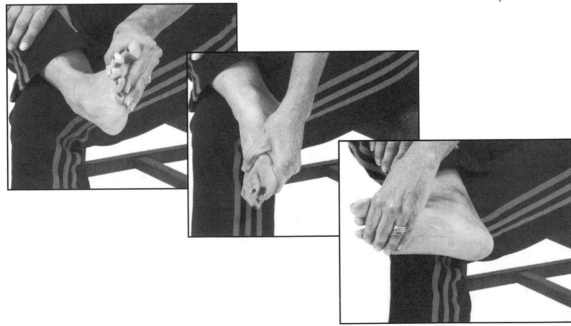

STARTING POSITION: Stand with proper posture. Extend your right arm in front of you to shoulder height, with your palm facing forward and fingers pointing toward the ceiling.

starting position

1 Gently pull your fingers back with your left hand until a desired stretch is felt under your wrist. Hold the stretch.

Repeat as recommended then switch sides.

1

ADVANCED

Try doing the exercise with the fingertips pointing down.

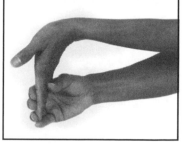

STARTING POSITION: Rest on your hands and knees.

starting position

1 Draw your belly button in, causing your back to round. Inhale deeply.

2 Now exhale and slowly relax your body to the starting position.

Repeat as recommended.

index

other ulysses press books

STRETCHING FOR 50+: A CUSTOMIZED PROGRAM FOR IMPROVING FLEXIBILITY, AVOIDING INJURY AND ENJOYING AN ACTIVE LIFESTYLE

Dr. Karl Knopf, $13.95

Details how to maintain flexibility, mobility and an active lifestyle by incorporating additional stretching into one's life.

WEIGHTS FOR 50+: BUILDING STRENGTH, STAYING HEALTHY AND ENJOYING AN ACTIVE LIFESTYLE

Dr. Karl Knopf, $14.95

Shows how easy it is for a 50+ person to lift weights, stay fit and active, and guard against osteoporosis, diabetes and heart disease.

YOGA FOR 50+: MODIFIED POSES & TECHNIQUES FOR A SAFE PRACTICE

Richard Rosen, $14.95

As baby boomers pass age 50, problems with knees, ankles and backs are leading them into lower-impact forms of fitness. Tailored specifically for this burgeoning population, *Yoga for 50+* offers a straightforward approach that makes it easy to learn yoga at any age.

BALANCE TRAINING: STABILITY WORKOUTS FOR CORE STRENGTH AND A SCULPTED BODY

Karen Karter, $14.95

This book takes balance training to the next level by offering a full range of exercises, including those incorporating cool, new pieces of equipment such as the balance cushion, the BOSU, and the Reebok Core Board.

BELLY DANCING FOR FITNESS: THE ULTIMATE DANCE WORKOUT THAT UNLEASHES YOUR CREATIVE SPIRIT

Tamalyn Dallal with Richard Harris, $14.95

A healthy aerobic workout that adds dancing, exotic music, the twirl of silk and the rhythmic clanging of finger cymbals.

ELLIE HERMAN'S PILATES MATWORK PROPS WORKBOOK: STEP-BY-STEP GUIDE WITH OVER 200 PHOTOS

Ellie Herman, $15.95

Explains how props such as the magic circle, small ball, foam roller and balance ball can enhance Pilates.

ELLIE HERMAN'S PILATES WORKBOOK ON THE BALL: ILLUSTRATED STEP-BY-STEP GUIDE

Ellie Herman, $14.95

Combines the powerful slimming and shaping effects of Pilates with the low-impact, high-intensity workout of the ball.

FIT IN 15: 15-MINUTE MORNING WORKOUTS THAT BALANCE CARDIO, STRENGTH AND FLEXIBILITY

Steven Stiefel, $12.95

Fit in 15 details a unique, full-body fitness program that even the busiest person can work into a morning schedule.

FORZA: THE SAMURAI SWORD WORKOUT

Ilaria Montagnani, $14.95

Transforms sword-fighting techniques into a program that combines the excitement of sword play with a heart-pumping, full-body workout.

FUNCTIONAL TRAINING FOR ATHLETES AT ALL LEVELS: WORKOUTS FOR AGILITY, SPEED AND POWER
James C. Radcliffe, $15.95
Teaches athletes the exercises that will produce the best results in their sport by mimicking the actual movements they utilized in that sport.

THE MARTIAL ARTIST'S BOOK OF YOGA
Lily Chou with Kathe Rothacher, $14.95
A great training supplement for martial artists, this book illustrates how specific yoga poses can directly improve one's martial arts abilities.

PLYOMETRICS FOR ATHLETES AT ALL LEVELS: A TRAINING GUIDE FOR EXPLOSIVE SPEED AND POWER
Neal Pire, $15.95
Provides an easy-to-understand explanation of why plyometrics works, the research behind it, and how to integrate it into a fitness program.

TOTAL HEART RATE TRAINING: CUSTOMIZE AND MAXIMIZE YOUR WORKOUT USING A HEART RATE MONITOR
Joe Friel, $14.95
Shows anyone participating in aerobic sports how to increase the effectiveness of his or her workout by utilizing a heart rate monitor.

WEIGHTS ON THE BALL WORKBOOK: STEP-BY-STEP GUIDE WITH OVER 350 PHOTOS
Steven Stiefel, $14.95
With exercises suited for all skill levels, Weights on the Ball Workbook shows how to simultaneously use weights and the exercise ball for the ultimate total-body workout.

To order these books call 800-377-2542 or 510-601-8301, fax 510-601-8307, e-mail ulysses@ ulyssespress.com, or write to Ulysses Press, P.O. Box 3440, Berkeley, CA 94703. All retail orders are shipped free of charge. California residents must include sales tax. Allow two to three weeks for delivery.

about the author

KARL KNOPF, author of *Weights for 50+* and *Stretching for 50+* (Ulysses Press), has been involved with the health and fitness of older adults and the disabled for more than 30 years. A consultant on numerous National Institutes of Health grants, Knopf has served as advisor to the PBS exercise series "Sit and Be Fit," and to the State of California on disabilities issues. He is a frequent speaker at conferences and older adult wellness events, and has written several textbooks and articles. Knopf is the founder/president of the Fitness Educators of Older Adults Association and the founder/CEO of Keep Fit over 50, an organization for wellness-minded baby boomers and beyond. He also coordinates the Adaptive Fitness Therapist Program at Foothill College in Los Altos Hills, California.

acknowledgments

It is with sincere appreciation that I thank Ulysses Press for understanding that vintage adults can grow well, not old, and that we are an important segment of the active adult community. Nick Denton-Brown allowed me to move in a new direction. Lily Chou took my raw thoughts and transformed them into smooth, flowing concepts. Claire Chun and Steven Schwartz's attention to detail made my concepts become a reality. Much appreciation goes to photographer Andy Mogg and models Toni Silver and Jacques Rutschmann, who were able to put these words into action. I'd also like to thank my family, especially my wife Margaret, whose patience allowed me the time and space to sit and write, and my sons Kevin and Chris. A special thanks goes to all the vintage athletes who continue to show me that age is in the mind and if you don't mind, it doesn't matter.